The Memory Of Broken Things:

And Other Stories Of Amsterdam And The Mohawk Valley

The Memory Of Broken Things:

And Other Stories Of Amsterdam And The Mohawk Valley

Dave Northrup

Mountain Air Books

Mountain Air Books
Scott Krause
1045 University Ave., Ste. #2
Rochester, NY 14607
585-442-9468
Email: Scottkny@yahoo.com

ISBN: 978-1-626-20259-7

Acknowledgements

Versions of some of the stories in this collection have been previously published in Voices de la Luna and halfwaydownthestairs.net

The author wishes to thank the following individuals and organizations:

Azar Nafisi, for permission to use the quote from her memoir *Reading Lolita In Tehran*.

William J. Kline and Son and The Amsterdam Evening Recorder for the front cover photograph, and the photographs on pages 57, 103, and 104.

Bruce M. Northrup for the photograph on page 56.

Mark Perfetti of MarkPerfettiPhotography.com for his technical advice.

My wife, Janet, for her unflagging encouragement and support.

In Memory Of Matthew M. Orante

PREFACE

It is an abiding fact of human nature that we are shaped by the place we call home. We carry it with us always, no matter how far we may travel from the locality of our birth and upbringing. My home is Amsterdam and the eastern Mohawk Valley of upstate New York. The settings and characters of the stories that make up this collection are fictional accounts of an imagined past. They are, as the French writer Albert Camus says, "the lie that reveals the truth."

First I hear the bell, a pause, and the closing of the street door. Then I hear footsteps coming up the winding staircase and past my mother's apartment. As I move towards the front door, I register a piece of sky through the side window. Each girl, as soon as she reaches the door, takes off her robe and scarf, sometimes shaking her head from side to side. She pauses before entering the room. Only there is no room, just the teasing void of memory.

Azar Nafisi, *Reading Lolita In Tehran*

Contents

THE VALLEY

The Memory Of Broken Things

Frankie remembered. Every Wednesday afternoon during that empty summer following his father's passing he'd sit quietly in the living room listening to his maiden aunts' worrying over his future. Immense in their formless black dresses, the two women stationed themselves at the dining room table wondering aloud what imp of perverse affection could have driven their youngest sister Rosie, so tall and robust, so full of the life of their parents' Fort Hunter dairy farm, to marry Jake Gardinier, a slightly built, timorous clerk from Amsterdam. Their braying whispers sounded clear in Frankie's memory.

"Well, Jake was always apologizing for something or other," one would begin.

"S-sorry to intrude, s-sorry for that, s-sorry to bother you, but… ," the other would mock his father's stutter.

"Jake never seemed able to face whatever life threw at him. Why, he was always bowing and scraping before all creation!"

"Sure hope Frankie don't turn out like his dad, Rosie. Why, the boy is so shy and quiet. And small for his age, too!"

In the silence following the women's judgments would come the squeaking of his mother's chair. Then he'd hear her voice, louder than her sisters' yet with a slight hesitation as if she were a bit unsure of herself.

"Well, still waters do run deep. My Frankie's a bright boy, but some kids are just bold and forward … and … others … are not. Looks like my Frankie is destined to be a thinker, not a doer. That's just the way he's made."

And always when his aunts were about to leave, he would be called into the dining room for a hug.

"What a love. What a darling boy! But try not to be so quiet and shy, Frankie. Don't be so timid!" they'd admonish, each in turn opening her pendulous arms to receive him. Frankie's breath always caught at the heavy fragrance of their perfume which had never been quite strong enough to hide the sharp sour smell of their seldom washed clothing. Well, they were both long dead now.

In the pale light of early morning Frankie looked about the interior of his car. On the floor in front of the passenger's seat lay what was left of the old mattock, its long handle broken into several jagged-edged pieces. The raised grain of the dried wood shone a dull grey and the tip of the dark rust-pitted pick was bent upward nearly an inch. It had been his father's. Memory often speaks in the language of broken things, and the old tool began to tell Frankie the story of a few weeks passing. He'd swung the mattock high as he could, expecting the pick to bury itself deeply in the soil beneath the old cherry tree. Instead he'd hit solid rock sending a painful shock back along his arms, and he'd looked down to find himself holding the broken handle with hands that felt like they were made out of jelly. Then he'd become conscious of the slow descent of the white cherry blossom petals he'd struck in raising the mattock so far above his head. Frankie had looked up to see a large clump of torn flowers and knew there'd be fewer of the fruit to harvest before the crows came to plunder. Fewer opportunities to savor the tartness of the small barely ripe cherries. He could not remember ever having tasted a cherry from that tree that had come to its full sweet flavor unravaged.

"Just like you always do. Go off half-cocked. For the life of me, I just will never understand why you can't ever seem to keep your mind on the business at hand," his mother had called to him from where she'd stood in the shade of the back porch.

Then he'd had to kneel and use the adze end of the mattock to scrape away at the rocky soil. It'd been hot work in the bright Spring sun. All the time his mother had stood over in the shade, the round black hatbox tied with white butcher's string at her feet. After Frankie'd labored to dig the hole deep enough, Rosie, holding the box by the string, had marched up and thrust it toward him.

"Well, she lived a long time. Twenty-three years is a damn great age for a cat!" she'd declared. The sun, high in the noon sky, cast a shadow accentuating his mother's lantern-like jaw, almost too pronounced to be a woman's. She'd looked down at him with wide-set eyes, unblinking.

"I think I'd like to get a small gravestone ... or something ... to show where she's buried," he'd offered

His mother's jaw had set, then slowly her mouth shaped itself into a derisive grin.

"Jesus, Frankie. You're thirty-five years old, not twelve. Act your age. It's just a cat. You spent enough money on her the last six months. Let that be her testament."

Dropping the cardboard coffin at his feet, Rosie had turned on her heel and marched back toward the house.

After he'd placed the box in the shallow hole and scooped the rocks and dirt back in, Frankie had stood and looked off toward the old horse barn in the Dirsie's backyard.

The white pickets of his mother's garden fence shone harshly against the chalky red of the barn's clapboards. The colors began to shimmer and blur together. All we are and all we have pass through our fingers like grains of sand. Who had said that? Some poet probably. Frankie had looked down, searching, and finally found two flat, fist-sized stones. He placed one on top of the other over the filled-in hole. No one would really know that they had been set there on purpose. He'd stared down at the stones blinking until his vision cleared and then had made his way back toward the house.

Frankie Gardinier opened the car door, picked up the pieces of the mattock, and swung about. The pick caught the pillow he used to prop himself up behind the wheel. Down it went onto the dusty floor. He grabbed the cushion, shook it, flipped it clean side up and placed it carefully on the seat. Then he made for the back of the garage, his shoes crunching on the layer of grit. He laid the mattock's remains in the old wooden chest, gently lowering the top to avoid raising a cloud of dust that otherwise was sure to settle on his dark suit and shoes. Back behind the wheel of the car, he adjusted the pillow again so he could see out the rear view mirror.

Carefully Frankie backed the car onto the gravel of Cory's lot. Luckily he had the third garage in from Columbus Avenue, not one of the ones around toward the back of Cory's house. He could back right out onto a thick layer of gravel and so avoid both the mud that much of the lot turned into whenever it rained and the dustbowl that it became in dry weather. Of course, he did pay extra to be closer to the street, but that was ok because he always had to look his best for work. It just wouldn't do to show up at the Men's Department of the Boston Store in the Schenectady Mall with his shoeshine dulled and his trousers spattered with mud or dust.

Worked too hard to get that job to let a little something like where he garaged his car get Ethel Blaustein thinking that maybe she'd made a mistake in hiring Frankie Gardinier.

He had to make the most of what scant assets he had. He knew that. He was short, and heavyset. But if he dressed in very tailored dark suits and blazers--absolutely no "natural shoulder" cuts for him!--he could appear thinner and taller. Of course, everything had to be sharply pressed, jackets, slacks, shirts, and all solid colors, no patterns, definitely not. Frankie Gardinier had to see an impeccably tailored, if portly, young man staring back at him out of his closet mirror each morning. Besides, he still had all his hair; and so far it hadn't lost any of its deep black color. He did have a heavy beard, that was certainly a plus. Although he shaved closely every morning, at noon he fancied that his face was darkened by the five o'clock shadow of a male in his prime. Yet his face was very round, the cheeks too full, mouth too small, and the chin receding.

Every morning in front of the mirror Frankie practiced stretching his mouth sideways in a cross between a grimace and a grin. He did this in hopes that it would make the lower half of his face appear broader and more attractive, more man-like. But in unguarded moments when he caught sight of his reflection, he saw only a swarthy-faced cherub staring back at him. Sometimes he felt he looked like a horrid parody of cupid.

It'd been hard enough getting a new position after he'd lost the job at Paley's Men's Shop in Amsterdam.

"It took me a damn long time to see I had no future with Al Paley, that's fer sure," Frankie muttered as he drove east on Columbus Avenue. "My God, the old man must've been seventy at least when I first started with him right outta high school."

That was another one of his problems, obviously.

"Can't see the big picture! Can't see the forest for the trees!" he could still hear his mother and her sisters harping at him years ago. He'd always paid too much attention to the details of the present, never planning for the long haul, caught up in a fantasy that one day he'd buy Al out and take over the shop.

He swung the car out of Columbus on to East Main. When he neared the city line, he gazed over at Coessens Park, once an elegantly manicured public garden stretching along the north shore of the Mohawk River. Before the war it'd had a swimming pool, picnic groves, clay tennis courts, and a couple of small white tiled bath houses whose front entrances were framed by fluted concrete columns. The baths were gone now, as were the courts. Large slabs of rubble-strewn concrete marked their passing. The pool had been filled in and the garden beds had turned to hummocks of sand and weeds. Frankie turned away, and guided the car out onto the Schenectady Road.

Surprised when Al Paley had suddenly announced his retirement last summer, Frankie had at first decided he should move out of Amsterdam and build on the experience he felt he'd gained at Paley's. "Why not go big?" he'd asked himself.

First, he tried downtown Albany. Had a damn hard time finding a parking place when he went for the interview. Thought for a while he'd have to hoof it all the way down to Pearl Street from Washington Park. But then he did find a place on the street just outside McManus and Riley. Boy, that was a beautiful day. Bright Fall sun casting knife-edged shadows between the tall buildings along State Street. He'd felt real confident, taken his time pretending to study the displays in each of the four large windows while every now and then glancing through the heavy cut glass of the door to see how many customers and salespeople might be on the floor.

"Welcome to McManus and Riley."

The tall, elegantly dressed salesgirl had approached fifteen or so minutes after eyeballing him when he'd first come through the door. No rush. We know you wouldn't be here unless you were comfortable with what we have to offer. Plush green carpeting on the floor. The woodwork was all dark oak and mahogany. There was even a mezzanine at the back behind an ornate iron railing where the pricier suits were kept. And the ceiling above the main floor must have been twenty feet high! This was the sort of place that had clients, not customers.

"I'd like to see the manager, if I may."

"And who shall I say...?" the girl had cocked her head to one side as she had looked down on him, a smile playing about her full, brightly painted lips.

"Frank Gardinier. I'm here to inquire about the prospects for employment."

"Oh." The smile stayed, and her chin rose and then dropped ever so slightly in acknowledgement.

"Just a moment, please." She had turned and walked away from him, her hips swaying invitingly.

The manager had appeared, an older, balding fellow not much taller than Frankie. He sported a sharp, pencil thin moustache and wore a severely tailored dark double-breasted suit. Frankie remembered with awe the impeccably executed Windsor knot of his heavy red silk tie. The manager had held himself erect, aloof from Frankie, but the tone of his voice had seemed open and accommodating.

"Have much experience in retailing men's wear, do we?" he nodded.

"Oh, yes. I've been in retail with a small full service proprietorship for almost twenty years. I also have experience marking up for minor alterations--cuffing slacks, shortening sleeves, dropping shoulders on coats, that sort of thing."

"Oh, we have our own in-house tailor do all that," the manager had said, quickly waving a hand in Frankie's direction.

Then, "A small proprietorship? And where would that be?"

"Amsterdam," Frankie had nodded. "Older fellow's retiring so I'm looking about for a position with a recognized, well-established firm where I can use my experience and, of course, learn more."

"Amsterdam! Why ... you'd make the drive down here every day?"

"Well, it's not all that far on the Thruway."

The manager's gaze slid from Frankie's face to a point somewhere at the front of the store.

"Tell you what. Let me take your name, address ... and phone number, of course. We have nothing right at the present moment, but I'll drop you a line, or give you a call, if something does come up."

Then he'd tried Lafayette's in Schenectady. It wasn't downtown Albany, and the clothing was a bit edgier in terms of style and color, but it wasn't discount, either. The walls were all bright blue and yellow with chrome racks glaring in the pitiless florescent light. He'd faced a young sales clerk who at first had stared open-mouthed at him. Finally the kid had blurted out, "Sorry, have everyone we need."

The morning sun striking the windshield gave promise of a warm day. East of the rock cut at Hoffmans, the Schenectady Road opened up to reveal low hills spreading gently up and away from either side of the Mohawk. To the southeast Frankie caught sight of the jagged blue peaks of the Helderbergs shimmering in the distance. He grasped the top of the steering wheel with both hands, pushing himself up and back against the seat, and began remembering the course of events that had brought him to the Boston Store.

After Lafayette's, he'd given up looking for awhile. He'd had six months yet on his unemployment not counting the eight hundred in severance Al had given him. At first he'd tried to spend his time doing odd jobs for his mother. But every time he'd suggest some project, she'd make the same abrupt reply,

"Frankie, it's a small house. If I need something done, I can do it myself. Been doing it for as long as I can remember, anyway."

Then she would sigh and add quietly, "Besides, you're not good with tools, you know that."

It was as though she did not want to change and had decided she would go on in her own way forever. So, he'd begun to spend his days walking about the shrinking city, often wandering empty streets among the vacant carpet mills, remembering the crowds that had thronged the lanes and alleyways of his childhood. Near the empty buildings he would hear again the rhythmic thunder of the giant looms and the raucous voices of the mill hands calling to one another at the open doorways. In the evenings he'd listen to the radio. The countdown of the top forty or fifty songs of the week, or month, or year would set him dreaming of the future. He'd imagine the jobs he might get in some yet to be discovered store in the heart of downtown Albany, or Manhattan, even. No longer alone in Amsterdam, he'd find his life and love in the center of a purple world of rich men and glittering women. But then certain memories would creep into the dream. He'd hear again the shouts of "pumpkin", his nickname in school, see again the derisive glances of boys he'd thought were his friends and the wary looks of girls he'd found attractive. He remembered once trying to confide his fears and sorrows to his mother.

"Well, Frankie, don't let the stupid talk of other kids get you down. You've got to learn to give as good as you get. Don't just hang back and take it! They're bothering you because they want to know what you're made of. Stand up for yourself! Remember, harsh words can hurt your feelings, but silence will break your heart! Somebody'll meet you halfway, and be your friend. Don't give up!" But he had given up. A line from a Shakespeare play he'd read in high school kept resounding in his mind, "Absent thee from felicity awhile." Others had moved on. He seemed broken, stuck in place, unable to move.

Then one evening he'd noticed an ad in the help-wanted section of the Schenectady Gazette:

> Help Wanted: Retail sales.Mens, Ladies, Appliances. 21 Big Depts. Apply in person. The Boston Store. Schenectady Mall.

For the interview he had sat at a table and filled out a job application blurrily mimeographed on paper through which the ink of his fountain pen bled remorselessly. Undaunted, he'd written large, holding the nib of the pen lightly to the paper. Then a thin, mannish-looking woman wearing a dark business suit had swept into the room, seized the application and planted herself in the chair across from his at the table. Ethel Blaustein had looked up from under grey bangs to study him. Frankie returned her steady look. Finally she spoke.

"You live in Amsterdam?"

The memory of the manager at McManus and Riley had flashed before his eyes. His aunts' harsh whispers sounded in his ears.

"Not a problem. I'm moving to Schenectady this week," he had nodded decisively. "That's why I'm here."

Ethel had stared at him, then launched into a lecture about the necessity of being on time, the importance of weekly sales quotas set for each of the twenty-one big departments, and the extensive surveillance system operating in the inventory rooms through which one had to pass to get to the employees' cafeteria.

"The only people I've had to fire in my twenty-four years here were those that were caught pilfering on their way to and from break."

She had looked at Frankie unblinkingly.

"OK," she'd said, "we're willing to take a chance on you." It seemed to Frankie that she had put too much emphasis on the "we're" and "you" as though maybe his hiring had more to do with the store meeting some sort of quota for the handicapped, than it did with any personal assets he'd presented. Nonetheless, he'd gotten the job.

It was just eight-thirty when Frankie reached the wide, four-lane bridge at Scotia and crossed over the Mohawk River into Schenectady proper. The sunlight beat through the windshield making the perspiration rise along his arms and chest beneath the dark suit coat. He cranked down the window, switched on the vent fan and the radio.

The speakers made the guitar instrumental sound tinny and far away at first, but then Frankie recognized the singer. Low, thick, and sweet as honey that voice slipped into him. Yet in the sweetness of that voice there was a twang as tart as unripe cherries. It began to cry out a desire undiminished by loss. The tempo of the guitar, piano and drums increased to a rollicking pace and the voice became an insistent throaty rasp. It fairly screamed, "I'm calling my lover, calling my man, ... calling my lover just the best I can." Frankie knew that call, understood that cry: the aching, driving need to find, and to be found. That voice gave the lie to the refrain, "Freedom's just another word for nothing left to lose." There is no freedom where there is such terrible desire, he thought.

Frankie got to the corner of Daisy Lane at eight-forty five, just in time to see a parade of students on their way to the local school. He didn't mind having to stop when the crossing guard, a short squarish woman in a long blue trench coat and what looked like a police cap, jumped into the street, arms akimbo, shielding her charges from the oncoming traffic. This morning the kids were talking excitedly, turning their heads from one to another as they ran across the street. They reminded Frankie of his own delight on long-ago magical spring mornings such as this.

He got to the parking lot of the Boston Store and cruised directly to the employee section. Frankie palmed the steering wheel with one hand, bringing his car right up to the curb, exactly straight in its space. On his left squatted Armand Capossi's aging dinosaur of a Lincoln Continental, sitting so low to the pavement that Frankie could see clear over its roof.

Armand was his co-worker in Men's Wear. In its size and outward appearance Frankie thought Armand's car matched the man. He must have weighed well over three hundred pounds and was at least a head taller than any other employee in the twenty-one big departments. All of Armand's weight was concentrated in the lower half of his body, and Frankie saw him as a fellow who lived his life close to the ground that bore him. He was a giant mama's boy. Every day, Armand would carry on a monologue about the virtues of his mother's love. He had lived with her for all of his forty-seven years, and could not imagine a life shared with anyone else. Spreading his soft, childlike hands on either side of a massive paunch and straightening his narrow shoulders, Capossi would roll great, doglike eyes toward Frankie.

"Why, Saturday night, Saturday night, Ma made us the most wonderful *due tiramisu semifreddo* followed by an *espresso corretto.* There is no love like a mother's love, eh? What that woman wouldn't do for me, and what I wouldn't do for her!" he'd stabbed the air with a pudgy finger. During these speeches, Frankie focused his attention on the stack of register slips or else pretended to straighten up stock.

Frankie swung round the corner of the open door to the break room, reached up to grab his time card, and plunged it into the slot at the top of the clock. He looked over to see Armand sitting alone at the nearest table, cradling a cup of coffee between his small hands.

"Good morning, Frank."

"Morning, Armand. Ethel around?"

"Somewhere. I saw her come in after me, but then she scurried off...something about ...inventory adjustment."

Armand's dog eyes stared up at him for a moment, but Frankie couldn't read any meaning in the glance. He walked slowly past the bulletin board on the wall, pretending to read the workman's compensation notices, smudged and flyspecked, scattered across the pitted cork.

Ethel swept into the Men's Department at five to ten with the cash drawer cradled protectively against her chest.

"Hi, guys," she said as she unlocked the register and slid the drawer into place. Putting her fingers on the front of the machine, she snapped the drawer closed with her thumbs then looked up at Frankie and Armand.

"Ok. Punch in your ID's and the two of you can go to work. Corporate has its eyes on the sales quotas for Menswear. If we can't improve the numbers by sharpening the pencil, we may have to make some personnel adjustments."

Ethel stood behind the register watching Armand and Frankie. It was the first time Frankie had seen her so still and quiet.

"Anyway, I need you guys to get started on inventory so we can make room for Fall stock. Just give me a sheet with a break down on size, quantity and price. Start with the slacks and sport coats.

She turned and marched off, the staccato of her heels echoing like gunshots in the silence of the empty floor.

"Wow," said Armand, "I guess the only certain thing is change, eh, Frank."

Frankie saw the mattock's broken handle, and the rubble of Coessen's Park.

"Yeah, I believe in change," he said quietly.

"Look, Frankie, why don't we start with the slacks and I can make out the breakdown sheet. You read off the stock."

Frankie smiled. He could hardly refuse, what with Armand's girth effectively preventing him from ever seeing his shoes, let alone being able to bend down to read the tags on the pant rack.

"No problem, Arm," he said.

The morning passed void of customers. The recorded music, seldom interrupted by chimes calling a manager or security, settled numbingly about the two clerks. Armand stood unmoving at one end of the pant rack, his arms stretched forward over his paunch to reach the pad of paper on which he wrote. Frankie's head bobbed down and then up as he knelt to see the sales ticket of each garment. He rose again and again to turn and call out the size and price to Armand. Frankie took comfort in the repetition. The sound of "36, 10.95", "36, 12.95", "38, 10.95", "38, 12.95" echoed in his mind like the slap and drag of the wipers on the windshield of his car, and beneath the sound of his voice ran the subdued rhythm of the store's muzak. He felt he had entered a dream world. Armand's size and immobility made him seem like some gigantic other-worldly presence hovering in midair. He looked like a genie just released from the magic bottle.

Frankie finished one side of the rack. He rose, stretched his shoulders and neck, looking away from Armand. When he looked back, he saw the first customer of the day standing to the left of the genie. She was blonde, and as tall as Frankie felt himself to be. She had an open, smiling face, appeared close to his own age, and was not spare in the neatly compact figure of a girl, but shapely in the ample flesh of a woman.

"Hello," her bright voice broke the silence.

Frankie made his way toward her.

"What can I do for you?" his smiled answered hers.

"Well, I'm really just looking," she giggled a bit. "I wasn't really intending to buy anything today."

"That's ok," said Frankie. "Hey," he laughed, "if you have a question, just ask. That's what I'm here for. It's really no bother. In fact," he lowered his voice confidentially, leaning ever so slightly closer to her, "I haven't worked here that long and probably need the practice talking about the merchandise and perfecting my sales pitch."

"Really?" she laughed openly as though relieved by his offer of help. He felt her light brown eyes resting gently on his face.

"Sure, I used to work at a really small store over in Amsterdam. But the owner retired, so, here I am, trying to do my best here. You see, I need the practice."

She didn't reply, and moved away, walking slowly about the department, looking first at the shirts, then at the socks, ties, the sport coats. Frankie, whose eyes followed her as she went, noticed that she kept looking back in his direction. Finally the blonde started making her way back to him, and he, consciously squaring his shoulders, stood still where she had left him, waiting for her return.

"You know," she ventured, "It's all so confusing. I think I'm going to get a gift certificate, so I can come back and look again."

"Great," said Frankie. Then his joyful confidence dipped a bit, remembering that, after all, this was Mens Wear and she was here to get something for a father, or a brother, ... or someone else.

"What name shall I put on the certificate?"

"Oh, I'll give you my name. That way when I come back again, you'll have had more practice and can help me make the right choice."

She looked at him, the open smile dimpling her cheeks that began to color with a faint blush. Her gaze slid from his eyes and came to rest focusing on a point somewhere in the distance beyond his left shoulder. Frankie looked closely at her face, at the strands of fine blonde hair turning to grey in places at the temples, at the delicate crows feet beginning to blossom near the corners of her eyes. Her smile began to fade, resolving itself when she drew her lower lip in slightly. He could see the narrow glint of her upper teeth as she bit delicately at the lip. She took a half turn, and glanced away, waiting. Armand had disappeared. The floor was devoid of customers. And Frankie Gardinier, hearing a rollicking melody, a honeyed voice as tart as unripe cherries, stepped toward her.

Red Wheelbarrow

The early morning sky above Schoharie Valley hung heavy with storm clouds. Thick mist lay about the lowlands obscuring all but the silo of Kurtz's small dairy farm. The fog bank rose high at the north end of the valley, its grey fingers reaching up to curl about the red brick clock tower of the Mariaville School. Gustav Kurtz pushed open the screen door of the kitchen, stepped wearily out onto the porch and into the wet blanket of thick air. In the early June morning the barnyard below him was a brown sea of thick mud. Rivulets of water, silver ribbons against the chocolate surface of the nearly liquid earth, flowed from the bottom of the manure pile off to his right. He marveled at the rainbow colored streaks that dappled the surface as the rippling water caught the rising sun's slanting rays. Stumbling down the stairs he set his boots nearly ankle deep into the muck.

Wind-driven rain had fallen most of the night, but just after daybreak the torrent had stopped. Now the air was calm as Gustav struggled toward the barn imagining he could feel the warmth of the cows reaching out to cling about his face and bare arms. Just outside the door he did feel their heat and breathed in the thinly sweet fragrance of hay before a heavier, sour stink reached him. In the spring especially it settled oppressively about the place, blighting the lush colors and delicate textures that blossomed at winter's end. Cow shit and rancid milk burdened Gustav's life. Try as he might, he could never completely wash those smells from his clothes and skin.

He stopped to stare at the manure rake propped against the rotting door jamb, then he turned and looked back at the house, its white clapboards black-stained from the narrow eaves down to the broad planks that skirted the roughly laid fieldstone foundation. His gaze circled back to the barn. Years of weather and neglect had turned the red paint a mottled purple and brown. The whole building looked like a bruise on the brightening landscape. Instead of washing away the grime and excrement, the night's storms had made the farm uglier, covered it with water come from all the sewers of the world.

With his older brother Bernie gone off to the war in Korea and his father laid up with a badly infected thumb, most of the farm chores had fallen on Gustav's shoulders. His mother had her hands full with the house and tending the chickens and kitchen garden while trying to nurse his father back to health.

At seventeen, Gustav was handsome and proud, with a square chin, pale blue eyes and a thick mane of nearly white-blond hair which he carefully combed into a sweeping pompadour. He was big for his age too, already nearly a head taller than his father. He had a man's voice and temper to go with it, just like the old man, who'd survived being a Wehrmacht infantry officer in the war.

"Whyn't ya go tuh th' doctor when yuh first cut the thumb in the barn?" he'd yelled at his father over a week ago.

"Vas? Wer's got th' money tuh go tuh th' damn doctor? You got it? An' who th' hell are yuh tuh tell me vat I should be doin?" The elder Kurtz started for his son, but then sat down abruptly, shivering as beads of sweat covered his forehead.

In the barnyard, Gustav stared down at the brown muck. The sun was out full force now, and he felt he was inside an oven full of rotting meat. Grasping the rake, he caught sight of his hands. He kept his nails cut short, trying to make it easier to wash away the traces of manure. Gustav looked at his palms and fingers, each crease and split seemed filled with traces of light brown filth that he would never scour away. Always that sourness clung to his hands.

He tore his eyes away and looked off to the right beyond the barn past his mother's garden. His gaze sought the wide mouth of the valley as it opened up to the freedom of the world beyond the farm. But all he could see was the clock tower jutting above the fog bank that still shrouded the school building.

He remembered bits of a conversation he'd overheard in the lunch line at school. It was last Fall and he was behind two town girls he'd been keeping an eye on. The one next to him he especially liked to watch. The way her dark hair caught the light and her eyes flashed excitedly when she turned to look about the classroom never failed to catch his attention. He didn't dare look at her face now. Just standing close to feel the warmth of her body and hear the sound of her voice would be enough. The girls were looking down at their trays, talking. Gustav strained to hear them over the noise from the kitchen and the shouts and laughter that echoed off the yellowed tile walls and floor.

"Oh, yeah, him." said the one.

"What?" said the other. Then the first one said something that sounded to Gustav like "cute" or maybe "Kurtz."

"Uh, uh. I don't wanna git touched by shitfingers, that's fer sure." said the girl standing next to him.

Her friend glanced up and saw Gustav. She blushed, lowered her eyes, and turning, moved quickly away toward the tables while the dark haired beauty next to him hurried after, calling, “Hunh? What? Where’re yuh goin so fast?”

Gustav threw the manure rake at the barn wall. Its long handle bounced off the planking and landed in the yard, throwing up brown spatters. Then he turned and ran toward the garden, his eyes seeking to take in as much as he could of the valley that was still hidden by the fog. Short of breath, Gustav stopped when he reached the two line electric fence that kept the cows away from his mother’s vegetables.

He stood, his eyes tearing, his thoughts clouded with the impossibility of ever knowing one of the town girls, of ever breaking free from the farm, of ever washing away the shit smell that made him part of the vile earth that clung to his boots. He looked round desperately and his eye caught a burst of color against the bare ground in front of the chicken coop. Stumbling toward it, Gustav saw a toy wheelbarrow, once his, that his mother had planted with flowers she’d nursed from seeds in late winter. Blossoms of white, pink, and dark violet nodded gaily above the bright red of the barrow’s freshly painted wood. Beyond, a few chickens, their snow white coats bright and clean, moved cautiously about.

Gustav walked closer, staring at the wheelbarrow. Its surface was lustrous with raindrops; it shone with a diamond’s million points of light. He bent down, reached out his hands, and gently wiped at the glaze of rainwater. Again and again he passed his hands over the red paint, his palms squeaking along the surface, feeling as though he were gathering fistfuls of coldfire crystals. He held his shining hands close to his face, breathing in the cool fresh scent. Through his fingers he saw the red wheelbarrow glowing beneath him.

Sans Souci

Jerry liked going to the movies. The Scotia Art Theater was just a couple of doors down from his flat over Nance's Hardware on Main Street. Actually, none of the few people he knew in the village of Scotia called it Main Street. It was the Amsterdam-Schenectady Road, and every two blocks through downtown there was a set of traffic lights, alternately timed so that all day and often at night a slow stream of cars and trucks passed under his front bedroom window. During warm summer nights when the sash was up and the drape pulled back, he'd lie in bed watching the reflections of vehicle lights move fitfully across the walls and ceiling. The glimmering reminded him of the flickering light in the theater just before the sound came up on the preview trailers. It was a kind of magical radiance that flashed out, illuminating for a second or two the faces of Mirth and Sorrow that were painted across the theater's walls.

Yeah, Jerry thought, living so close to the Scotia Art was a real plus. To get there he didn't have to put up with the hassle of clanking along over the uneven asphalt with the canes and leg braces to get to his car out back. Nope. He could just bang down the wide stairs from the second floor then make his way over the broad level sidewalk to the movie theater. There he could imagine moving effortlessly among the figures on the screen. He was one with them as they talked, walked, ran and jumped, spoke with eloquence, anger, desperate passion … and took each other in their arms. Yessir, he had a lot to be thankful for. At thirty-four he could get about on his own and had a job with Andy so's he was independent and didn't have to live in a home or anything like that.

The May evening was warm, traffic unusually light on the street. The quiet air was sweet with the purple scent of lilacs that crowded a small park just beyond the theater. Mary the ticket girl was already in the little booth fronting the sidewalk and slipped his ticket under the glass as he approached. She greeted him with a toothy smile and a bright "Hi, Jerry."

"Hey, Mare," he said propping a cane against the side of the booth while he fished in his pocket for the money clip.

"Here. Change is for you." He deftly slid a five across the sticky surface of the metal shelf .

"Whatja do? Hit a number?"

"Nah. It's just such a beautiful evening. It's great to be alive. Why not share the wealth? Ya know?"

"That's my boy," she grinned. "Always willin' to share. Enjoy the show." Mary looked down on him through glasses as thick as bottle bottoms, her round face framed by a straggly mass of blue grey curls.

"You enjoy the quiet out here, too. Ain't every night's as peaceful as this one's startin' out to be," he nodded at Mary as he grabbed his canes and shuffled forward, the open doors of the theater inviting him in.

Jerry took his usual aisle seat a couple of rows down on the left. He got comfortable and looked about the theater thinking that there'd probably be a sparse crowd because it was so beautiful outside. Then it dawned on him that he'd clean forgotten to notice what the feature was. Well, that was ok. He did remember that the Scotia Art was running a Bergman festival, so he figured that what crowd there'd be would be older, more accustomed to nuance and detail, not looking for a lot of shoot-em-up action. Besides, in weather like this most younger people would want to be outside, seduced by the eternal mysteries of the soft spring night.

A couple holding hands passed Jerry. They were dressed in identical denim jackets and worn jeans and appeared to be headed for the short row of side seats far down in front. Jerry glanced at them and then riveted his gaze on the woman. She was a blonde, tall and thin who swung her shoulders in a restless way as she moved down the aisle. For a minute or so he thought she might be Terri Ambrose, the waitress over at Sans Souci, a restaurant across from Nance's where he liked to take his evening meal. But when she turned to take her seat he saw that this woman's face was roundish and pug-nosed, where Terri's was lean with a slightly hooked nose and square jaw. Although she moved with the same kind of restless energy, to Jerry's relief, she wasn't Terri Ambrose.

Lately he'd begun to think about Terri a lot. She'd only been at the restaurant since last December and was maybe ten years older than he was. He liked to joke around with her. The usual banter.

"Hey Jerry, my favorite customer. What'll it be tonight?"

"I'm all yours. I'll be havin' whatever you suggest this evening. I trust you completely," he'd invariably reply.

One night, he remembered, she'd changed her greeting.

"How ya feelin?"

On the instant he decided to take a chance, be a bit daring.

“Hah. Not much anymore,” he gave her a broad smile and looked directly into her large blue eyes. Smiling, she’d returned his look, slowly nodding as if in approval,
and Jerry could see that age had begun to make its inevitable marks in the wrinkles around her mouth and eyes. But she was still attractive. Instead of being borne downward as many women were, the years and her circumstances had seemed to pull outward on Terri making her appear angular and lean. He remembered one time when her old Nash had broken down, he’d given her a ride home to her apartment over on Lefferts Street after work. She’d thanked him and then slipped out of the car so quickly he hadn’t a chance to say good night.

The house lights dimmed as the curtain parted noisily. Jerry propped the canes against the seat to his right, pushing himself up as straight as he could. Even before the screen lit up, the music crackled harsh and dissonant from the speakers. When the darkly lit sky above a rocky, desolate coast appeared Jerry knew the feature would be *The Seventh Seal*. His spirits sank a bit. Beyond the walls of the theater, the warm darkness was alive with the promises of life, but in here he knew the movie would make him feel surrounded by another kind of darkness that he didn’t want to think about, for there was no need to, not yet anyway. Jerry waited a bit for his eyes to grow accustomed to the gloom, and then quietly rising, moved toward the door to the lobby.

As he passed Mary, he looked in her direction, “That flick’s too depressing for me on a night like this. See ya later on in the week.”

She returned his words with a wan smile and a slight nod.

Jerry made his way back to Nance’s building. The scent of lilacs still lay heavily on the air, and the traffic had picked up some. All the parking spaces along the street in front of the Sans Souci were filled, as were the narrow lots on either side of the building. When he reached the street door to his second floor hallway, he paused and turned, looking at the restaurant. The front was wainscoted in black tile from the sidewalk up to the large curtained windows that framed the recessed entrance. Above the windows and all the way to the roof the façade was silver colored with horizontal ribs of metal backlit by pale blue neon. The ribs curved back around the sides of the building. Centered in the middle above the doorway was "Sans Souci" written in a flowing script of glass tubing. The name glowed a rich neon pink against the metallic blue background. The place shone like the prow of some great ship plowing through the velvet darkness of the night.

Jerry struggled up the stairs, entered his flat and went straight to the front bedroom where he pulled the curtain open and pushed the window up. The street had quieted some. He took a deep breath of the sweet night air and looked out at the people and cars moving to and fro beneath his window. The scene brought memories of warm nights back in 1946, just after he had turned fourteen. Nights he'd spent propped before another bedroom window, the lower half of his body lying useless behind him. He watched former playmates running and jumping under the glowing lights of Carmichael Street in Amsterdam. Once in a while some of the boys would look up and call out to him and he'd call back, but he knew even then that he'd never again be able to move as they did. As for the girls, well, none had even looked in his direction. It had taken a while, but he'd finally understood the lack of interest there. As he'd grown older, and managed with the leg braces and canes, his hands had become strong and sure. They had taken on the energy and grace denied to his legs. He had come to take a delight in precision and detail. In the final year of high school, he'd learned the trade of printing, so he could make his way in the world.

And he did have his collection of music. It had started with a few records of the symphonies of Brahms and Beethoven played over and over on the second hand phonograph his parents had gotten for him shortly after the polio had struck. One Christmas he'd received the Great Moments in Music album and discovered the works of the French Romantics. Their music let him imagine a life in which he could go anywhere and do anything.

Jerry made his way to the living room where he sat in the straight-backed chair before a small table on which he'd put the old record player. He turned on a small lamp and bent forward, shuffling through the stack of albums on the floor until he found the Gabriel Faure. When the sensuous melody of the Pavane began rising about him, Jerry sat back, raised his chin and looked toward the open door to his bedroom. There, reflected from the front of the Sans Souci, the light shone a pale blue and pink. The music flowed over him. He reveled in the wave of anticipation the melody suggested, following it note by note until the tender end. Then he picked up the canes and went back into the bedroom where he stood before the open window looking at the soft glow across the street.

It had taken a long while, but he'd accepted his lot. He knew only two things. You cannot change the past, and the future is all anticipation. Tomorrow always follows and then, why, anything might happen! Feeling a surge of strength course through his hands and forearms, Jerry grasped the canes tightly. He felt he could stand at that window looking down on the restaurant all night.

It was ten o'clock when the kitchen at the Sans Souci closed. By that time, the lots across the street were mostly empty, and soon, Jerry caught sight of Terri Ambrose heading for her car parked under the street light in the space closest to the sidewalk. She was alone and walked quickly, with arms folded protectively across her chest. The old Nash started with a roar, blue smoke belching from its tailpipe, and he watched as she craned her neck about to get a better view of the oncoming traffic before heading the car out onto the street. He caught sight of her face. Terri's lips were parted crookedly as though she found it hard to breathe. Below the mane of blonde hair, a deep wrinkle worried her brow. Her face looked like a study in distraction and vulnerability.

Turning from the open window Jerry sat on the bed, removed his leg braces and lay back fully clothed. He watched as the pale reflections of light from the street moved across the ceiling and walls of the bedroom. They looked like the warm glow of Christmas lights shining into his door-less bedroom long ago. His eyes grew heavy with sleep. For a while all was quiet until he heard the harsh murmur of angry voices. He knew the sounds of his parents arguing in the living room. The discord had blossomed each night of that Christmas season after the summer he'd gotten sick. He could not hear the exact words spoken, but the sharp bitterness in their voices filled his ears, and then he heard Terri Ambrose's voice. It had the same edge to it when she'd told him about her son, Nick, autistic, and committed to Mt. Loretto in Albany.

"Yeah, when the father found about his little darling he took off pretty quick," she'd confided to Jerry. "But…so…you gotta accept what you can't change. That I've learned the hard way…." Her voice had trailed off.

The next morning dawned in a hot yellow haze. By the time Jerry made his way out to the car in the lot behind Nance's, the collar of his shirt was clammy with perspiration. Working the hand throttle and brake, he drove east over the Western Gateway bridge into Schenectady. Turning right from Erie Boulevard onto Bridge Street he guided his car into the small lot next to Andy's Gateway Print Shop. The place did small contract printing jobs for the town of Scotia, local businesses, and customers who walked in off the street. When he reached the counter Jerry saw Andy Martuscello, the proprietor sitting on a high stool in front of one of the letter presses that stood along a wall in the rear half of the shop. Andy looked up owl-eyed behind his glasses and peered at Jerry.

"Son of a bast. S'gonna be a hot one today, for sure. Hey, I can't get this goddamn page locked. Here … you come here and do this. Knapp is comin' in this morning for the business cards and picnic flyers and I got other stuff I gotta take care of."

Andy hopped down from the stool and limped stiffly towards the counter. He was barely five feet tall, rotund, with sparse grey hair fringing his shiny bald head. The black boot on his left foot had a sole several inches thick and as he walked it rapped loudly on the uneven planks of the wooden floor. Jerry made his way over to the press and sat before it, quietly surveying the crooked lines of metal type Andy had tried to lock into the press chase.

He selected the right size furniture to square up the page. Then he locked it all down and started the press, deftly inserting and removing the folio sheets as the machine hummed along. The poster was for the Scotia police department's annual PBA picnic. When that job was done

Jerry moved over to a smaller press to do sheets of card stock for the investigators' business cards. As he was cutting the sheets, he heard Andy stomp up behind him. Jerry turned to watch Andy inspecting the stack of posters.

"'Atsa nice job, nice job. I just can't seem ta get them galley's lined up lotsa times. 'An besides, I'm scared ta death of that damn press when it gets ta goin' fast."

Jerry gave Andy a satisfied smile.

"Hey we're a good fit fer each other, right? My hands might be quicker 'en yours, but your feet move a lot better than mine do," he said.

Shortly before noon Knapp the beat cop from Scotia strode through the door. He wasn't in uniform, but even though Jerry was way back at the press, the instant he glanced toward the front he knew who it was. At six feet five and with his bug eyes, short hair and lantern jaw, Knapp bore a remarkable resemblance to Frankenstein. In spite of his appearance and his job though, Knapp was an easy-going guy. In all the time Jerry had spent around downtown Scotia, he could not remember Knapp ever raising his voice or acting in anger or haste.

"Here you go. All done just like you order."

Jerry watched as Andy leaned across the counter handing the wrapped posters and cards up to Knapp.

"Hey Jerry. How's it goin?"

"Good to see you today Officer Knapp. You look especially handsome out of uniform, especially on this scorcher of a day."

"Aww, it's nice of ya to say that, Jerry. Yer my guy, and I hope to see ya at the picnic. We need more upbeat citizens like yourself around."

"Well, it ain't fer over a month yet, but I have every intention of being there."

"Yeah, I know, but the Chief wants th' posters early this year. Community relations an' all that, ya know," Knapp smiled back at Jerry.

"An' I know yer a man of yer word, so I'll look forward to yer presence," Knapp called back as he vanished through the door into the mid day heat.

At closing time Jerry made his way through the heavy air to his car. The second shift at GE was just letting out. He was worried that he'd have a hard time getting to the bridge over the Mohawk what with all the rush hour traffic and the other drivers made irritable by the heat. But when he got to the corner of Bridge Street, the driver of a delivery truck waved him on, so he slipped right into the line of cars coming up Erie Boulevard. And when he got into Scotia and had to turn left into Nance's lot, a woman in the oncoming lane smiled at him and slowed down so he could turn in front of her. These small mercies gave him a renewed energy. His canes and braces didn't clank as much as usual when he ascended the stairway. In his bedroom Jerry saw the lights of the Sans Souci glowing crisp and cool across the street, and decided to change into one of his Sunday shirts before heading over for dinner.

It was a Thursday and early so the place was pretty empty. Squeak the lanky bartender with the high-pitched voice had his back to the entrance and stood staring up at the large neon lit clock above the bar. Angie the hostess and Terri were standing before the doorway to the kitchen with their backs to him as Jerry maneuvered to his usual booth. Once he got settled, he looked over at the two women and Angie started in his direction. He noticed that Terri hadn't turned round.

"Hi, Jerry Kuchina. How's our best customer?" Angie chirped, carefully laying the plastic covered menu before him. She peered at him through glasses whose rhinestone encrusted frames were shaped like truncated batwings. Angie's face, framed by a mass of black curls, was covered by a thickish layer of makeup and she'd sharply defined her lips in deep scarlet.

"Enjoy!" Angie flashed an impish grin.

Jerry gave her a broad smile and nodded appreciatively. He watched her go, gliding away in her tight skirt and high heels. His eyes rested a moment on Angie's upper back. The right shoulder blade was thrust far out creating a bulge in the tight fitting jacket. Her left shoulder sloped noticeably lower than the right.

He looked down studying the menu and suddenly Terri Ambrose was next to the booth. She stood very still gazing down at him.

"Well, what'll it be this evening?" Her red-rimmed eyes gave the lie to the smile that forced itself across her tightly drawn lips.

"Why… whatsa matter?" he blurted out.

"It's nothin', Jerry. Just the usual with Nick. Everybody's got problems, right?

"Sure, everybody's got problems. Lord knows I got 'em myself," he glanced down at the tabletop on which the menu rested. "But sometimes other people kin help. Ya know, talk to somebody you think can understand. Look, just get me the special an' afterwards, if you want to talk about it, I'll be here. Looks like it's gonna be a slow night anyways," he offered, trying to glance over at Squeak who was still polishing glasses behind the bar.

A desperate desire that she trust him rose in his breast. He found it difficult to breathe and looked up into her blue eyes.

"Please, I want to help you in any way I can," he said.

"Yeah, ok. We'll see. If it ain't too busy," she whispered, casting him a sidelong glance before moving off toward the kitchen.

Jerry looked down at the knife and fork lying crossed on the empty plate, his mind a jumble of memories of Terri's face and phrases from the small talk they'd shared since she'd started at Sans Souci. He unfolded the check she'd handed him with the dinner. He'd half expected a note saying they could meet somewhere after she got off work, but it was just the bill for his dinner. Her handwriting looked childlike, the letters and numbers large, round, and uncertainly drawn. Jerry reached for his money clip and drew off three twenties for the dollar ninety meal. He folded the bills in half, with the check over them. He sat watching as the dinner crowd thinned out. Then Terri appeared from the kitchen. She made her way toward him hesitantly, as if the tables and chairs between them were obstacles she found difficult to maneuver around. Her shoulders were hunched, and she seemed a pale frightened thing that needed protection.

"Well, here I am." She slipped into the seat opposite him.

"I'm here to listen. I want to help, in any way I can," he said softly, placing both his hands on the table before her.

"Yeah, well, it's really nuthin' all that unusual. You know Nick's got a lot of problems. He just has never been able to communicate like other people can. Plus he's got this physical problem that keeps coming back … over the years …."

Her voice outran her breath and she fell silent a moment.

"So, he has this shunt, see. It drains fluid from the brain. Sometimes it doesn't work and he gets really bad and they have to do a procedure on him to clear it."

She stared into Jerry's eyes and the restless energy seemed to come back to her. She raised her hand gesturing across the table at him as her voice grew louder.

"Look, Nick ain't gonna die from this. It's just that the surgery costs money, an' it takes him longer and longer to bounce back each time it happens. An' it's always gonna be this way. It ain't ever gonna change. We're just gonna go on like this until the end."

She kept her large eyes on him, her face working in a mixture of grief and defiance.

"And I'm damned tired of it, is all," she said quietly letting her hand fall gently back upon the table.

"I want to help you, any way I can," Jerry said earnestly.

"Th' Terri an' Jerry show, huh?"

She drew her shoulders up, moved back in her chair, placing her hands together in her lap.

"That ain't your place, even if you do want to help. Oh, no. I done things I ain't proud of, everybody has. But all that's over and done with now, anyways. Besides, the people that should be helpin' ain't done nothin' in over twenty years now."

Her angular face with its high cheekbones and prominent chin lost its animation and became mask-like.

"People don't ever change, and they are never forgiven," she said quietly.

Jerry drew the bills wrapped in the check from his pocket, placing them on the table. He hesitated and then said, "I don't want nuthin' for it."

Terri took the packet without looking at it and retreated into the kitchen. After a bit Jerry rose. Grasping the canes, he started for the door. Angie came up behind him.

"Hey, Jerry. I got your change here," she called.

He turned and took a step toward her.

"Naw," he shook his head and smiled, "that extra bit's for Terri."

"No, she says it's not."

"Yeah, well, it's th' tip."

"No, Terri says thank you, but it's not the tip. And you're not to argue with her, she says."

"Ok, ok. I'm not pushing myself on nobody."

Angie, unsmiling, stood as though blocking him should he try to return to the booth. She handed him the bills and coins, and he swung around and shuffled toward the door.

Out on the sidewalk the humid air was painful to breathe. Jerry found it difficult to concentrate and had to look several times before he realized that there was no traffic to hamper his crossing the street. Looking to the east, he saw *Wild Strawberries* lettered across the marquee of the Scotia Art, and decided that sitting in the dark coolness of the theater might help him sort out all that had just happened with Terri. When he got to the ticket booth, he slid the dollar-fifty under the window without looking up at Mary. Instead of taking his usual place, he settled into an aisle seat in the first row at the back. The movie started. When the image of the handless clock filled the screen, Jerry began to think that maybe time for him was running out. As he watched the story unfold, the air in the theater began to feel as hot and oppressive as that which he'd left behind on the street. He feared ending up alone and adrift like the old man in the movie. By the time the film ended, he knew that he could not bear any gulf between himself and Terri Ambrose.

When Jerry got up to his flat he put the Pavane on the record player, and listened carefully to what the music told him. He decided that with just the right words he could make Terri understand. The next evening he was at the restaurant early. Angie brought him the menu and then came back to take his order.

"Where's Terri," he asked.

"She's takin' some time off. You know why," Angie replied matter-of-factly.

"Sure. Listen, I feel kinda funny about the conversation we had. I just want to square things with her."

"Oh I'm sure she understands that, Jerry. But, she's takin' some time off. We don't really know when she'll be back. Now we gotta hustle to find a fill in for her. So, we're movin' on. Maybe you should consider doin' the same."

Jerry ate his meal in silence, and left a generous tip for Angie who was scurrying from table to table by the time he left. His bedroom was quiet except for the occasional drone of traffic rising from the street below. The sense of urgency that had gripped him in the theater the night before would not let him go. Somehow he had to find a way to let Terri know that he meant her no harm, that he only wanted to help in whatever way he could. At length he decided to write her a letter. It would have to be brief, to the point. He did not want to take up a lot of her time with long-winded explanations. He'd apologize if she had misunderstood his intentions, and then end with another offer to help. He decided to put his return address on the envelope to show her right off that he was above board, that he wasn't trying to hide anything. The next morning he gave the letter to Andy to mail when he went over to the Schenectady post office.

Jerry felt a sense of relief, and decided to lay off going to the Sans Souci for a while. He felt sure that Terri would respond quickly, and let him know when she'd be back at the restaurant, and what help she'd need from him then. Every day when he got home he checked the mailbox, but after more than a week without even a note from her, the old urgency seized him, so he decided to write again. This time he asked if she might like to go to the PBA picnic in a few weeks and included some of the strips he'd cut from the Sunday comics "just to cheer her up," he wrote. More days passed, and still the mailbox remained empty, so he decided to withdraw a hundred from his savings account. He mailed the five twenties in an envelope without a return address. When no reply came, he decided to drive by her apartment house. He turned the corner onto Lefferts and saw her Nash parked on the street right in front of the entrance to the block. The car appeared empty, so Jerry slowed down to get a good look around. As he approached, the driver's side door suddenly swung open and Terri stepped out. She turned to face the oncoming traffic and looked directly at him. Her eyes went wide. She slammed the door, hurried around the back end of the Nash, and ran toward the building.

That evening not even music could lessen the desperation that bore down on Jerry. He knew that Terri wanted nothing to do with him, but he could not rid himself of the desire for some sort of connection with her. That she must know.

"Terri," he wrote, "I would do anything for you, to have any kind of a relationship with you. A relationship on your terms."

It was after seven on a Friday night two weeks later. Sans Souci was busy. Jerry had to stand in line behind four couples before he confronted Angie at the hostess' station.

"Hey Jerry, I got a booth way back that's just clearing out. Give us a minute and we'll get you settled, ok?"

Jerry looked around. There were two new waitresses, nondescript brunettes barely out of their teens, who were scurrying from table to table. He decided to go over to the bar and see if Squeak knew anything about Terri.

"How's tricks there, Squeaker? Looks like ya got a good dinner crowd tonight." Squeak looked steadily down at Jerry. It took him a good minute to reply.

"Jerry. Haven't seen you in a while. What brings you here?" The falsetto sounded strangely subdued, as if Squeak were trying to share a secret.

"Well, it's the great food, of course!"

When Squeak didn't respond, Jerry leaned close to the bar.

"Look, I've been trying to get in touch with Terri, and we can't seem to connect and I was wonderin' if you might have heard anything? "

"What, who now," asked Squeak.

"You know who. Terri Ambrose. Waitressed here fer Chris' sake," Jerry said, raising his voice a bit. Squeak stared down at him.

Defeated, Jerry offered, "I just want to get in touch with her is all."

"Uh, yeah, sure, I guess you do, but I can't say if she's gonna be back. It really ain't up to me, ya know."

Jerry was about to reply when he saw Angie standing at a booth along the back wall waving at him.

"Sorry to bug ya," he said quietly to Squeak and started toward Angie.

Jerry sat facing the entrance. Every table was taken and he looked around for one of the waitresses. He noticed Squeak bending down to talk to Angie at the bar, then they walked through the doorway into the kitchen. Finally one of the new girls came over and dropped a place setting and a water before him, murmuring that they were really busy and she'd be right back. Jerry passed the time by focusing on the clock above the bar. As he watched, the second hand seemed to sweep faster and faster around the bright pink dial. When he looked down, he saw that Squeak was back behind the counter, but Angie was nowhere to be seen. Finally the waitress came, took his order, and disappeared again. Jerry sat gazing vacantly around. The line of people waiting to be seated was still several couples deep and the drone of voices from adjacent tables began to make him drowsy. He closed his eyes briefly. When he opened them he was surprised to see Officer Knapp in uniform, maneuvering around the waiting customers, headed straight for the bar. Close behind Knapp was another fellow dressed in sport coat and tie, who looked like a businessman but moved with the quick agility of an athlete. Squeak and Knapp exchanged a few words, nodding at each other, and then Knapp turned, looking around the restaurant. Jerry raised his hand and waved, but evidently the officer didn't see him, instead bending down to talk to the guy who had followed him in. Then Knapp turned and left. The athletic looking guy sat down on a barstool with his back to Jerry.

Just then one of the brunettes brought his dinner over and Jerry started in on the blue plate special wondering what might have brought Knapp into the restaurant in the evening. He ate slowly, thinking about how the Sans Souci had changed. It was really busy, and now even the police in uniform were coming into the place. Over the last two weeks, he'd come to accept that he'd never hear from Terri Ambrose again, and now he understood that he didn't have a place here anymore either. He'd leave a good tip and walk out with a smile. It was ok, really, but he knew the hurt would last.

Jerry crossed his knife and fork over the empty plate and looked up to see the guy who'd come in with Knapp approaching. The closer he got, the broader he seemed. Sitting down, the guy placed his elbows on the table and clasped his hands together. The muscles in his upper arms outlined themselves under the material of the sport coat.

"We have to have to have a talk, Jerry," he said in a voice loud enough to make sure he was heard over the low din of the restaurant.

"Do I know you?"

"You will after our conversation."

"What," said Jerry.

"The letters have to stop."

The fellow passed a small card across the table. Jerry picked it up. There was something vaguely familiar about the color and texture of the thick paper. He looked down at the printing and read the bold script, "Thomas K. Emery, Scotia Police Department, Bureau of Investigations." Jerry didn't bother reading the rest. He knew there was an address and phone numbers listed on the bottom because he remembered the job he'd done for Knapp several weeks before at Andy's.

"The letters have to stop. The letters to this Terri," Emery said. He hesitated a moment, eyeing Jerry steadily. "This Terri Ambrose. The letters are just too upsetting."

Jerry's mouth felt like the desert, but he swallowed, took a deep breath, and managed a steady look at Emery.

"It was a mistake. An awful mistake is all. I just wanted to help. I just got carried away, is all. I ain't sent nothin' in over two weeks. It won't happen no more," he said.

Investigator Emery sat quietly staring at him.

"What about the money?"

"I won't send any more money, either."

Emery sat silent.

When Jerry spoke again, his voice was slow, deliberate.

"I just wanted to help. I just want to help people if I can, anyway I can. Ask anybody that knows me. That's all."

The investigator leaned across the table.

"Look, Jerry, this isn't a criminal offense. The lady just doesn't ever want to be bothered again. She doesn't want trouble, you don't want trouble, and I don't want you to have trouble. I just need you to give me your word of honor there won't be any more trouble. No letters, no money, no driving by her apartment, ever again."

"I will never bother her again."

When Emery made no reply, Jerry pushed the card back across the table, but the investigator, not taking his eyes from Jerry's face said in a clear voice,

"No, no. You keep it. To remember."

Jerry looked at his handiwork.

"Nice clean printing job on your card," he said.

Emery looked at him quizzically. Jerry stood, dropped a small handful of bills on the table and gave the investigator a vigorous nod. Then he took the canes and started for the door. Once out of the restaurant he stopped. The early summer evening was eerily quiet. He looked up. Above the glare of the street lamp, the starless sky was a deep blue velvet. Jerry Kuchina thought of the cool darkness of the Scotia Art Theater, how you could always count on the scenes and characters on the screen changing. If you didn't like one flick, you just had to wait awhile for the feature to change. There were always new stories coming along. All you had to do was wait for them to arrive.

RAILROAD

Atlas
TAVERN
Atlas TAVERN
RESTAURANT

The Gandy Dancers

"Awright, Tim, gimme me that tie plate here."

Eddie Geiger's voice rumbled in the damp morning air like the roll of distant thunder on a still summer's night. The grey canvas overall he wore would have hidden the limbs of lesser men, but on Eddie great slabs of muscle outlined themselves beneath the cloth covering his forearms, thighs, and upper back. His left foot was braced against a railroad tie, the right thrust behind him while his hands were raised above his head and wrapped about the end of a long steel bar levered beneath a section of rail.

Tim, the black man, lithe as a cat, danced up to the track and stepped between the ties, his thickly soled jack boots crunching in the gravel of the ballast. At waist level he held a large flat piece of steel.

"Yes, suh," said Tim, his voice tight with the strain of his burden.

"That's right, that's right," rumbled Eddie, his face a catalog of contradictions colored by the exertion of pulling down on the bar. Veins bulged, coursing like great pink snakes along his neck. Above his upper lip the once sharp edges of a pencil-line mustache had begun to blur into the indistinct smudge of several days' growth of beard that shadowed his cheeks. Eddie's forehead was smooth, the brow of a young

man of not more than thirty years, but his eyes had that hunted, vulnerable look that often comes with advanced age.

Tim Tibeau, broad-shouldered, narrow-hipped, wore a dark knit skull cap pulled down over the tips of his small ears. His eyes were large, the upper lids slanting down a bit at the outer corners, giving them a guarded look. Tim’s face was the color of coffee grounds and small dark scars pocked the skin over his prominent cheekbones. Tibeau’s history was written in his face and in his movement: he had been an amateur boxer before signing on with the New York Central track gang after the war.

Eddie grunted and cursed, yet the rail remained motionless at his feet.

"Where th’ hell is Bernie?” he thundered.

"Hold on, big man, here I come," a sing-song tenor floated above the crunch of jack boots on gravel.

"Bernie, grab th’ end of th’ pinch bar so's Tim can get th’ tie plate under," barked Eddie as he raised the lever over his head.

Bernie Andrulis, the tallest and thinnest of the three gandy dancers, reached above Eddie and grasped the end of the bar. For an instant the two men seemed suspended like giant bats; the skirt of Bernie's greatcoat spread out from his legs like half folded wings. Slowly they pulled down on the lever, and the end of the rail began to rise above the tie. The black man, squatting low, knew just when to pitch forward, letting the weight of his burden carry the tie plate under the rail. His companions held on to the pinch bar as the weight of the rail carried them both upright, their arms slowly ascending once again above their heads. When the end of the rail came to rest on the tie plate, they let go of the bar and Eddie turned to face Bernie.

"Where th' hell yuh been? Me and Tim been bustin' ar asses fer twenty minutes ta fit this plate." His voice was tight with anger and hurt.

Bernie raised his sparsely bearded chin. The reddish-blonde hair barely covered his jaws, as though he'd taken tufts of pig's bristle and glued them randomly to his skin. A blush began to cover Bernie's neck. It spread up over his cheeks and across the thin bridge of the sharp beak of his nose, making his face a kaleidoscope of pink and red blotches. He swallowed, and his Adam's apple, sharp pointed, worked up and down.

"I was in th' tool house checkin' spikes." The words, slowly uttered, were defiant, more a challenge to fight than an explanation.

"More like playin' with yer spike, than countin' New York Central's," smirked Tim.

Bernie clenched his fists and turned. He took a step toward the black man. Seen in profile, Bernie's face lost its incongruity of color and form. The nose thrusting downward and the thin chin hairs curving upwards gave the impression of a goat.

"Uh, oh. Uh, oh," laughed Tim, his eyes going wide. "C'mon whiteboy," he called out. "C'mon an try ta git a piece of the best nigger boxer in th' Mohawk Valley." He danced a bit from side to side, his fists pointing downwards, pumping at the air.

"That was nineteen-forty, this's forty-eight," Bernie shot back, the goat's chin nodding in Tim's direction, but he made no move to get within arm's length of the black man.

"Cut the shit, both a ya," said Eddie. "Yuh want ta play with yourself, Bernie, do it on yer own time, not on me an Tim's. I wanta git this section done before noon. Now go on back ta th' shed and git th' go-devil and th' spikin' hammer.

Th' pay office closes at one. We ain't workin' this afternoon, and we ain't workin' tomorrow."

"Ahh, Sunday, day a rest after Saturday night," sang out Bernie. "What's it gonna be t'night Eddie, beaver or booze, eh? Booze or beaver, what's it gonna be, Eddie? What's it gonna be?"

He turned and moved off down the track in the direction of the toolhouse, hopping from one leg to the other, his arms dangling between his legs in mimickry of an ape's stride. Tim turned and gazed openly at Eddie.

"Hope yuh ain't payin' many visits tuh th' tool house this mornin', neither."

Eddie turned away from him. Tim nodded slowly, the guarded look coming back to his eyes.

"Yea, he who wanders from the way of understanding will come to rest in the house of the dead," he said softly.

"He's just goin' back to th' tool house ta git what Ah told him to."

"Ain't him Ah'm worried about," said Tim.

The two men stood silent, avoiding one another's eyes and waited. After a few minutes the click and screech of the handcar reached their ears. They turned to see Bernie, bobbing up and down over the rocking arm. The fury of his effort made the skirts of his coat billow out from his legs. At a distance he looked like a scarecrow balanced atop a child's toy. As he neared Eddie and Tim, Bernie stood upright, grabbed the brake handle with both hands and pulled back, his mouth open and tongue protruding with the effort. The car shrieked slowly to a stop.

"One gen-u-wine, new-matic, nooky and nigger-approved New York Central spikin' hammer at yer dis-pos-al," Bernie squeaked in a harsh tenor, pointing at a tangle of hoses and bars strapped to the side of the car. He jumped down, his boots crunching on the ballast as he went over to a pile of tie plates Eddie and Tim had set near a rail.

"The two of yah start th' engine an git th' air up in the tank. Ah'm goin' back to th' house an' git a track wrench," said Eddie moving off quickly in the direction from which Bernie had just come.

Bernie flicked his tongue between his lips and glanced at Tim.

"Ah sure hope he don't make no mistakes that'll get my ass hurt."

"Well then," said Tim, rousing himself, "maybe yah just better watch your ass today."

The two men stared at each other.

"Don't get uppity with me. Ah like my fun, but at least Ah know when and where to do it so's Ah don't kill myself and maybe somebody else into th' bargain."

"Yep," said Tim.

Eddie stepped up to the sliding door of the tool house and paused, turning to look across the river. The sun had risen high enough to mark the four black smoke stacks of the Adirondack Power and Light generating station on the south side of the Mohawk with brilliant white lines along the edges where they curved away from his sight. Memory flashed the ruins of Koblenz before his eyes.

Spires and stacks, their outlines gilded by the rising sun, loomed above the brown rubble. Eddie felt again the weight of the BAR he held at his waist. Slowly he walked forward, swinging the barrel from side to side. He saw the sharp-faced girl with dark eyes standing before the black doorway. Eddie raised his hand toward the smoke stacks, and motioned for the girl to get back inside the ruined building. But she didn't move. She stood holding him in her dark doe eyes, a mischievous smile playing across her lips. She was his own age, he thought. Her meager shoulders were wrapped in a tattered black shawl which left her pale, blue-veined arms bare below the elbows. She held her hands clasped above the waist of the dirt-encrusted skirt that was long and broad and hid her feet. The girl was so thin, and the fabric of the garment so thick, that it did not show the usual folds and creases of the body beneath. Indeed, it was as though the skirt itself held the girl erect.

Holding him with those dark eyes, she bent forward at the waist grabbing the hem of her skirt with both hands. Slowly she straightened up. Eddie saw again her bare legs so beautiful and white, soft and smooth against all the pocked and fractured stone. Then he saw the glint of metal between the legs, and Eddie Geiger, without a second's hesitation, leaned forward into the recoil which he knew was coming, and which he knew had thus far preserved his life. He unloaded maybe half the magazine from the BAR into both of them there in the doorway. He heard the ragged echoing thunder of the gun and he saw the girl tumbling backwards atop the German's shoulders, those beautiful white legs kicking at the air. The landser's helmet flew off into the pink and grey cloud that enveloped the doorway.

Eddie Geiger shouldered the sliding door to one side and entered the toolshed. In front of him sat a workbench, its surface strewn with a few well-thumbed copies of girlie magazines. A large toolbox reposed on its bottom shelf. Eddie bent low, grabbed the box by the side handles and swung it up onto the top. Across the lid of the box was embossed in fat, authoritative letters, *The Gandy Tool Manufacturing Company, Chicago, Illinois.*

Quickly unlocking the padlock of the chest and raising the lid, he brushed aside a piece of dirty canvas which covered a large canteen. He took gulp after gulp until the canteen grew light in his hands and the hot breadth of the rye boiled out his nose, numbing his tongue and biting at the back of his throat. Then he took care to wrap the canvas sheet securely about the canteen and slowly placed it back in the chest. He knelt before the bench sliding the tool box back on its shelf.

Eddie emerged from the toolhouse and looked down the tracks. In the distance Tim and Bernie appeared small, insignificant figures. The big man lifted his gaze skyward. To the west, he saw the sunlight striking the tell-tale strung below the signal stand that spanned the tracks at Cranesville. The light shone brightly on the copper wrapped ropes hanging below the row of track lights. They seemed like red bars placed across the clear blue expanse of the morning sky. He turned and stepped off in the direction of Tim and Bernie.

The gandy dancers worked slowly. Tim's movement was a study in deliberation as every now and then he cast a look in Eddie's direction. Bernie's face was a mask of indifference turned away from his companions. Eddie, stupid with the peace he'd found in the tool house, stood stiff-legged keeping silent watch over them.

Suddenly conscious of his responsibilities as boss of the track gang, Eddie Geiger, throwing his shoulders back, looked up. Deep creases of resentment knitted his brow. His eyes took in his companions with a hard, belligerent stare.

"Gimme the ballast-tamper here," He bawled. "Ah wanna make sure the gravel is compact enough aroun' them plates yah bolted."

"Lemme do it, boss," Tim said quietly.

"Ahm' th' foreman! Foreman makes sure th' job's done right! Gimme the god-damn tamper!"

Tim dragged over what looked like a long shovel connected by a length of hose to the handcar. At one end was a round handle into which a crescent shaped hole large enough to take a man's gloved hand was cut. Fitted within the top edge of the crescent was the trigger. The shank of the handle became a wide cylinder below the point where the hose from the compressor was attached. From this cylinder jutted a heavy bar ending in a broad square foot. Eddie grabbed at the handle, pulling the tamper close to his side in an attempt to swing it over the rail. But his movements were slow and clumsy. His gloved hand wedged into the handle, jamming itself against the trigger just as the end of the tamping bar brushed the top of the rail.

Eddie heard the single ringing crack of metal on metal before he felt the gut-punch hit him high, just under the ribs. The impact rose through his chest, splaying out his elbows, rushing into his jaw, taking all his breath with it, propelling him into the air where he hung for an instant before the ground rose suddenly to meet him. Then he lay motionless between the rails. Bernie leapt the short distance to him.

He bent low, screaming into Eddie's ear.

"What the fuck are yah doin?"

Tim stepped to Bernie's side. There they stood, stock-still in the shock of what had happened. Wide-eyed, they stared down at Eddie, whose legs soon began to kick out against the ties on which he lay. Tim roused himself and spoke quickly.

"Hep me git him up. Ah'll hold 'im. You git the tamper back on the damn car. Th' hell with th' ballast. Let's get 'im into th' truck."

With Tim holding him up, Eddie lumbered forward. His head was bent down and his eyes took in only the ties and rails over which he slowly picked his way. With each step a dull pain pulsed deep within Eddie's chest, and when he mounted the low steps to the crew cab of the truck and started to swing onto the seat behind the driver, an agony tore at his lungs bringing before his eyes a vision of the black doorway in Koblenz.

Tim settled into the driver's seat. Bernie turned toward the tracks.

"Wait. Ah forgot ta lock th' god-damn rocker arm," he called back over his shoulder as he ran off in the direction of the handcar.

"Hold on, boss, we getcha ta th' hospital in Amsterdam."

"Ya take me ta th' pay office, first," Eddie said in a high, tight voice.

The truck's door swung wide, and Bernie jumped up onto the passenger's seat. Tim gunned the engine, and the truck lurched along the narrow dirt road leading to Route Five.

At the corner of Main and Bridge Streets, Tim swung the truck to the left, toward the train station. Bernie's head snapped toward him.

"Boss says we need ta git ar pay first."

Tim kept his eyes forward, studying the traffic swarming about the entrance to the station.

Bernie's lips slowly twisted themselves into a grin. Two large yellow teeth appeared in the middle of the pig's bristle.

"Whyn't ya let me turn in th' time book and git th' pay, boss?"

"Sure," grunted Eddie. He sat forward, grasping the back of the driver's seat, his eyes shut against the pain. Beads of sweat glistened on his forehead.

Tim brought the truck up next to the side of the station farthest from the passenger entrance. Bernie hopped from the cab, his coattails sweeping behind him. In the bright noonday sun he strode toward a half-open dutch door shaded beneath the broad overhang of the station's roof. He slapped the thin purse-sized paperbound time book down on the narrow shelf of the closed lower half of the door. Casey, the paymaster, a slight, narrow-shouldered fellow in a crisply pressed white shirt and perfectly knotted dark tie, looked up at the disheveled gandy dancer towering in front of him and then down at the book. His voice, thin and reedy, seemed to float up toward Bernie.

"Eh? Gang boss supposed ta present th' timebook fer pay, Andrulis," he piped out.

His face a solemn mask of unconcern, Bernie stared down at the little man.

"Gang boss is in th' truck," he said evenly, raising a hand to gesture over his shoulder.

Casey remained silent, head down, the thumb and forefinger of his right hand slowly caressing a dogeared corner of the timebook. It seemed to Bernie that the paymaster was prepared to wait all day for an answer that would let him hand over the pay envelopes. The goat's face contorted. Sharp lines cut across the forehead and pursed lips pushed forward above the reddish goatee. Slowly Bernie shook his head in exasperated disapproval as he leaned over the shelf confidentially.

"Well, ya see, th' foreman's got th' usual problem."

Casey looked up at Bernie. His small eyes glittered in the reflected sunlight like two black pearls. Before he spoke, he pulled his upper lip high, exposing a row of small white teeth.

"You tell Geiger he's ta be here eight o'clock Monday mornin'. Shuttleworth wants ta see him. You tell him, don't have the Roadmaster come lookin' fer him again."

The black jewel eyes held Bernie until he felt forced to look away, then Casey reached under the shelf and brought up three fat brown envelopes. He placed them carefully on top of the time book.

"Yes, sir. Ah will give him that message. Ah will tell him several times, yes, ah surely will, and thank yah, sir."

Bernie scooped up the envelopes and, bowing low, shuffled backwards away from the door, turned, and headed for the truck.

"Any problem?" asked Tim.

Bernie sat erect, staring to the front. Something in the distance had evidently caught his attention.

"Nah. Ol' Rat's Eyes Casey didn't say a damn thing. Ah just slapped th' book down and he gimme th' envelopes, after, a course, fiddlin' around tryin' ta find 'em. That's what took s'damn long."

Bernie sat back relaxed, expansive. He slouched low in the seat, his knees thrust up against the soot-colored metal dashboard. His left arm was draped across the backrest, passing behind Tim's shoulders. His other arm extended out the open window. He turned toward Eddie piping in a mocking tenor. "Waal, guess everthin' worked out ok, eh? Getcha to th' hospital right quick now. Don' hafta work 'til Monday. Ah gotta feelin' next week's gonna be a good week. Yeh, Ah really do." His lips twisted into a grin and his eyes settled on Tim who kept staring straight ahead as the truck moved slowly up Bridge Street toward the hospital.

Eddie's Story

Above the Mohawk Valley the heavens seemed at war with the earth. Strong winds lashed low scudding clouds across the spring sky, and over the crowded thoroughfares of Amsterdam immense patches of deep shadow routed broad swathes of bright sunlight. Through this chaos of light and darkness a yellow truck lumbered its way up Market Hill. The driver, whose face was as black as the bold lettering which proclaimed "New York Central Railroad" across the side doors of the vehicle, wore a dark knit cap pulled down over the tips of his ears, and his eyes, set above high cheek bones, were slanted a bit at the corners, giving them a guarded look. He kept a watchful eye on the crowds of people trying to cross in front of the truck each time the heavy traffic came to a halt. From his perch in the cab, the black man could see when the cars ahead began to move and would gun the engine in anticipation. The roar and greasy exhaust served as warning to the throng of pedestrians who jumped back to the sidewalks.

In the seat next to the driver sat a white man whose hair was an unruly mass of red curls. He was narrow of cheek with a pointed chin covered by a straggly amber beard. In profile the fellow appeared goat-like. He sat forward in the passenger seat as his restless eyes moved continually over the faces in the crowd below him.

Behind the driver the open window of the crew cab revealed a dark haired man. His upper lip and cheeks were smudged by several day's growth of beard, and if any of those taking their chances at trying to cross in front of the truck had looked up at this fellow, they would have been struck by the corpselike pallor of his skin and the large beads of sweat dotting his brow. He stared out of the window with such intensity that he seemed oblivious to the rush of all around him. His gaze appeared fixed not on the chaos in the street, but on some inward turmoil impossible to ignore.

"Yuh take me to Doc Vi-lyn's. I don't need ta go ta no hospital," the pale fellow mumbled in a deep bass.

"Whut?" said the black man, staring at the traffic ahead and trying to catch the words over the noise of the engine and the crowd passing in the street.

"Yuh heard me. I jus' broke a damn rib, is all. Don't bother tuh go to St. Mary's. Jus'take me to Doc Vi-lyn. Up on Division."

"Ain't smart, boss. Gotta fill out th' paperwork an' get you properly looked at. You was out for awhile. Besides, Vi-lyn… . " The black man's voice trailed off as he turned toward his red-haired companion in the front seat. The goat turned his eyes on the sallow-faced man, slowly appraising the drops of sweat spread across the forehead.

"Tibeau's gotta point, Eddie. What with th' insurance an' all, and Ahm' not sure ol' doc Vi-lyn's th' right guy anyway. This job might be a bit much fer him."

Eddie turned from the open window, his enormous hands had the back of the driver's seat clasped in a white-knuckle grip. He stared intently at the back of the black man's neck.

"Ahm th' God damned gang boss!" his voice rose, darkly menacing. Then he stopped, drawing short breaths, and when he spoke again, the voice was tight, as though he were using all of his strength to force the words from his throat.

"Bernie, you an' Tim are gonna take me to doc Vi-lyn's. Ah ain't goin' ta no hospital. Ah don't need no paperwork or people askin' questions fer that paperwork. Alls I need is tuh git taped, git some rest, an' git back ta work in a few days."

Bernie turned and looked forward raising his hands palms up above his head while a crooked yellowed toothed grin appeared in the pig's bristle beard.

"Th' big man gets what the' big man wants," he said.

Tibeau headed the truck a short way up Market and then took a left into a narrow street deeply shaded by factories and warehouses built flush against the sidewalk. As the truck headed west, the street and sidewalks gradually widened, the looming buildings giving way to stately homes fronted by ample lawns. The truck slowed to a stop in front of a low sign perched crookedly at the edge of an expanse of unkempt grass. The sign read, *N. Violiunas, Physician* in fancy longhand script. Bernie jumped from the cab and trotted around to the driver's side of the truck. His height allowed him to place his elbows on the edge of the rolled down window, and he leaned into cab, speaking quietly to Eddie.

"Whyn't yuh sit here while me and Tim go up first tuh see if Vi-lyn's around?"

"Ahm goin' in with the two of yuh," the big man's voice rumbled, but the menace was gone, replaced by a plaintive quality as though the speaker was beset by a burden almost more than he could bear.

Tim swung out of the driver's seat while Bernie opened the cab door as wide as it would go. They both reached in to meet Eddie's outstretched hands, and slowly pulled him from the truck. Tibeau draped one of Eddie's massive arms over his own shoulders while Bernie grasped the big man's waist. They slowly made their way up a long tree-lined walk toward the porch of a rambling Greek revival manor house. The wind made the light and shadow dance madly about the three, and billowed the skirts of Bernie's greatcoat. Huddled together they seemed like some primal beast slouching through the wilderness. When the gandy dancers had ascended the porch, Bernie detached himself and Tim let Eddie lean against the peeling paint of one of the house's square columns. Bernie pressed a bell button, and not hearing any ring, began to slap with an open hand against the heavy glass of the locked storm door. Time passed. The inner door opened revealing a sharp-faced, diminutive woman, her grey-blonde hair swept back tightly from the brow. She stood gazing uncomprehendingly at the goatish face and the wild red hair. Then her eyes took in Bernie's companions leaning against the pillar, and she began to close the door against him.

"*Juk tu pazisti mane! Esu Andrulis. Bernis Andrulis,"* he yelled in Lithuanian at her through the glass. Pausing between each word as one might speak to the deaf or demented, he shouted, this time in English, "Ah got a man with me. He's hurt, needs th' doctor."

The old woman looked up at Bernie, her fearful eyes scanning his face. Then came a flash of recognition, she nodded, raised a finger, and moved back from the doorway.

"Nick-o-lay, Nick-o-lay!" she called out in a shrill voice, turning her head toward the cavernous interior of the house.

Eddie Geiger sat hunched forward on the examining table in the dimly lit room. Tim Tibeau stood to one side of

Eddie while Doctor Violiunas, lost in a worn dark suit coat several sizes too big for his stooped shoulders, busied himself before a glass-doored cabinet at the head of the table. Bernie Andrulis, arms crossed over his chest, held himself aloof against the wall near the door. The old woman approached Eddie and carefully unbuttoned the coverall to the big man's waist. Quickly she and Tim extricated his arms from the stiff sleeves of the canvas. A grey metal flask disengaged itself from the inside breast pocket of the jumpsuit and hit the floor. It bounced once, high, before skittering along the dusty tiles and coming to rest at Violiunas' feet. The doctor turned quickly toward Eddie. The old man narrowed his watery grey eyes and pursed his thin lips, as if considering the clatter of the flask a symptom to be noted in the treatment of his patient.

Violiunas shuffled over to Eddie and carefully raised one of the gandy dancer's elbows. He squinted at the broad area of flesh that had turned a pale blue from waist to armpit, then guided the elbow down and stepped in front of the big man. The doctor raised both of his own arms to chest level and fluttered his hands up and down. They were small white birds against the dark caverns of his sleeves. He opened his mouth in an exaggerated show of inhaling.

"Breathe. In…in."

He placed a stethoscope on the front of the big man's chest.

With each breath a throb of agony pulsed in Eddie's breast. The pain moved up to his jaw and made him clamp his teeth against the urge to vomit. Violiunas moved the scope slowly around the torso. From his station by the door, Bernie began to speak.

"We all work on th' railroad. His name's Eddie Geiger. He's th' gang boss. Got hurt on th' tracks this mornin'. Air hammer bounced off a rail and caught him in the chest. As yuh kin see, he's a big guy but the hammer musta lifted him a couple feet off the ground. Anyway, he come down and was out fer a few minutes, maybe more. Can't say fer sure cause it took me and Tim here completely by surprise when it happened."

He paused and looked at Tibeau who stood silent and still as an ebony statue gazing down at the floor next to the table. Bernie gave his shoulders a slight shrug and continued.

"So he come to an' starts in about how he don't want tuh go tuh the hospital. Wants tuh see you instead tuh get taped. So we got 'im the' truck, stopped off at th' pay office, it bein' Saturday an' all, an' then come directly here, just like he told us to."

The old man's wrinkled, parchment-colored face was a study in concentration. He spoke slowly, shaking his head back and forth.

"Yah, yah…nuh. You must have x-ray. Broken rib at least, maybe more. Have to go to hospital."

Then he brightened, looked up at Bernie and nodded emphatically, "Hurt on job, have insurance to cover this!"

"It's just a damn busted rib. Ah wanna be taped, is all, God-damn it," Eddie hissed. He sat unmoving on the table. Tim stood silent next to him. Bernie remained against the wall, staring up at the high, cobwebbed ceiling.

"But anything could happen. Even with a big strong man like you. I tell you as doctor you must have x-ray! You must be observed for a while."

"Ah wanna be taped! Ah ain't goin' tuh no hospital," Eddie's voice rose, querulous, regaining some if its menacing depth.

"But it's not good, I tell you," Violiunas pleaded, his eyes flitted about the room like a small bird's, unsure of where to light. "Especially with the alcohol … " the old fellow's voice trailed off into a whisper.

"God-damn all a ya!" Eddie said, his head shaking slowly from side to side in anger.

Bernie, shifting his weight, raised his shoulders high against the wall without moving his gaze from the ceiling.

"Klasuyk! Po velniu," he rasped out in Lithuanian, then lowered his eyes on the doctor. He spoke slowly, holding the old man in his gaze, "We just got paid. We don't see no reason, so long's yah know what th' basic problem is, ta go ta no hospital."

Doctor Violiunas glanced apprehensively up at Bernie. The old man seemed to retreat further into the depths of his shabby coat. A wan smile of resignation began to play about his lips and he turned toward the old woman waving a hand in the direction glass-doored cabinet containing the rolls of surgical tape.

"Yuh kin drop me off at the Atlas after we settle th' big man with his ma."

Bernie was in a relaxed and expansive mood, slouched low in the seat, his knees thrust up against the soot-colored metal dash board of the truck. He piped in a mocking tenor.

"Waal, guess everthin' worked out ok, eh? We got paid an'got ya taped up so's yah kin move about easier. Don' hafta work 'til Monday." His lips twisted into a grin and his eyes settled on Tim who kept staring straight ahead.

"Yah. Well, me, ahm' gonna git some rest and re-lax-a-shun. Git me a few drinks. Ah might even be goin' pearl-divin' later." His goat's head nodded up and down decisively, then he turned further and leered at Eddie.

"Whut about you, big man, eh? A man in yer condition can't be drinkin' but yah might be able tuh do little pearl-divin' later tuhday, or tuhmorra, huh?"

Eddie cast a baleful eye at Bernie. The tape held him erect in the seat, kept his breathing shallow, and lessened the dull throb in his chest.

"Jus' drop me off at home, Tim," he said evenly.

Tim pulled into an alley just wide enough for the truck's passage, drove a short distance over cobblestones polished flat from wear, and stopped before a ramshackle porch attached to a two storey house of crumbling brick. At the sound of the truck, a curtain in one of the high downstairs windows was shoved aside revealing a tall woman, one hand on the hip of a drab-colored housedress, looking boldly out at them.

"Yuh need a hand, boss?"

"Nah," said Eddie, a bit of the deep resonance returning to his voice, "Ah'll see ya Monday."

Slowly he descended from the crew cab and moving stiffly erect around the front of the truck, headed for the porch stairs. Tim backed the truck down the alley and turned east on Main Street.

"On second thought, whyn't yah just let me off in front of Slezak's?" Bernie said quietly, staring ahead at the slow moving traffic.

Tim turned to Bernie. The guarded look in his eyes.

"Ah'd be careful of who Ah was seein' if I was you," he said.

"Yeah, well, by th' looks a things, maybe some people might not be too long fer this world. Ain't no harm in doin' a bit of plannin' ahead, as Ah see it," Bernie responded, his words slowly measured.

"Tuh study on the death of another be th' devil's work," said Tim, pulling the truck up to the curb in front of a tenement of dun colored brick. Bernie opened the door, stepped out into the chaos of sunlight and shadow, and then turned back addressing Tim.

"Ah gotta make my provisions gainst th' future, just like any other man," he yelled, but Tibeau sat silent, his face an inscrutable profile staring ahead. Bernie slammed the door, and quickly made for the entrance to the building. Once inside the cramped foyer, he scanned the rows of small buttons before pressing his thumb hard against the one above a neatly lettered nameplate reading "Payzak."

Bernie stood facing the inner door, its glass curtained on the inside. Although he knew that a stairwell lay beyond, the folds in the curtain made it impossible to see into the hallway of the apartment house. Nervously shifting his weight from foot to foot, he waited. The unexpected silence bore upon him and he pressed the button again. He jumped when the buzzer finally sounded. At the foot of the stairway, Bernie looked upwards, expecting to see Ida. But the second floor landing, darkly illuminated by a single bare bulb hanging from the ceiling, was deserted. Her absence told him he was not the visitor she was expecting, and he stood a long moment before mounting the stairs. Slowly he moved along the dimly lit corridor, the words of greeting he'd prepared slipping from his mind with each forward step. When he stood before her door he could think of nothing beyond the certainty that his knock would tell her there was a stranger in the hallway. As he raised his knuckles to the darkly painted wood, he struggled to think of how he might counter her surprise.

The door swung slowly in, and Ida stood before him in the bright living room, her green eyes already raised to meet his own. Bernie watched as those eyes grew wide in wonder and then quickly, in an attempt to mask her disappointment, dropped to a gaze level with his chest.

"Bernie Andrulis." It was statement of regrettable fact, as though she'd taken note of some minor misfortune, like the loss of someone else's pet or the expected passing of a remote acquaintance, which must be acknowledged before one could move on.

"Ida, we have tuh talk. It's about Eddie," he managed before he grew silent in apprehension of the effect his words would have on her.

"Eddie? What about Eddie?"

She took a half step back from him and raised her shoulders slightly, girding herself as if for battle. Bernie gazed down at her, taking in every aspect of Ida Payzak's appearance: the thick blonde hair cut short like a burnished helmet of bronze that framed her brow and curved down to caress the clean soft line of her cheek; the slight flex of muscle along her lean arms bare in the sleeveless blouse, soft white down on skin golden in the sunlit room; the shape downwards, spare yet puissant in the long close fitting skirt. Ida of the golden hair. Bernie stared at her and saw sapphire skies, deep green groves, and brilliant alabaster columns shining in an ancient, golden landscape.

"He got hurt. On th' tracks. Earlier this mornin'."

"What? Well, if it was that bad, it woulda been all over town by now," Ida turned her head a bit, regarding him askance. Her green eyes, narrowing, held him.

"Nah. We think he probably just broke a rib is all. Didn't wanta go tuh th' hospital. Insisted me and Tim take him tuh Doc Vi-lyn. And he did get taped up, but th' old man wasn't happy about doin'it. Started to raise Cain about not know'n what else might a got busted till we showed him th' color of ar' money."

Bernie stopped, unsure of how to proceed, knowing that he had reached the point at which he must surrender to the hold that Ida had over him. He could only let her lead now; perhaps she would take pity on him. Perhaps that was the way to her heart. Ida turned her back to him and spoke to the small kitchen area at the rear of the living room.

"Why did you take him to that quack?"

There was anger and blame in her voice.

"That's where he wanted us tuh take him."

"So yah do what ever he wants yah to? Whyn't yuh take him tuh the hospital so he could get looked at properly?"

"Ida, a man like that…."

She stood, tears filling her eyes.

"He was drunk again, wasn't he? That's why yuh didn't take him because if th' railroad finds out that it's goin' on again, they'll can him and you won't look so good either," she said in an agony of recrimination.

Ida looked back at Bernie. In the ever-changing light and shadow of her living room, she saw a chaos of gangly limbs and harsh colors. There seemed nothing solid about him, nothing she could ever hold herself to. Memory began to flood over Ida. She had known Bernie Andrulis, and Eddie Geiger, since those summer days of girlhood when her father would take her from Fort Hunter to Amsterdam to help sell vegetables and fruit in the narrow streets. Her older brothers were left behind tending the farm while she'd sit next to the old man as the small truck rattled along the wooden bridge over the Mohawk and sputtered its way up the steeply winding road into Tribes Hill. They would head east then, down the long incline into the city. On hot days her father would open the windshield and she'd sit still in her seat, the breeze cool and insistent against her face and breasts. The old man would work his way along the alleys near the river, and end up at his brother's house in the East End. There he'd spend what was left of the long summer day having black bread and beer, and speaking Lithuanian with her uncle, a childless widower. She'd sit alone on the porch looking down quietly at the other kids playing in the street. Ida remembered the summer when she'd first seen Bernie and Eddie. That summer when she'd become a woman, and saw the one, a sharp-boned, red-haired scarecrow, staring silently up at her; and the other, a dark-eyed, embarrassed presence who even as a boy seemed to have the shoulders of a man.

The memory held before her eyes as Ida made her way to the kitchen table. Sinking into a chair, she looked back at Bernie. He remained silent just inside the open door. In the instant their eyes met, each understood that a decision was to be made. Ida raised her chin, folding her arms about her chest, drawing herself erect in the chair. Bernie took a half step farther into the room, then bowed his head and turned, disappearing into shadows of the hallway.

Eddie moved forward, his eyes set on the porch steps before him. He heard the sharp creak of the front door as it swung inward, and looked up to see his mother standing, one hand on her hip, the other hanging at her side holding a lighted cigarette, its long ash dangling precariously. With each step he took, the throbbing pulsed within his chest, and to fight off the grey mist that hung threatening at the edges of his vision, he focused on the figure of Edna Geiger framed by the open doorway. His gaze rose from hands to face, taking in a bit of the room behind her. He was struck by the contrast between the woman who stood before him and the girl who gazed bravely out from the large framed wedding picture set atop the upright piano near the door. The dark eyes, so bright and prominent in the photo, were shadowed now, confined by deeply creased lids. The once dark hair, falling luxuriantly about the shoulders was now pulled back from the forehead in a greasy, grey-streaked bun, the finely cut nose had been transformed into a long and sharply narrowed beak.

"What's a matter? Didja get hurt?" his mother demanded, her eyes narrowing on him.

"Nah. Jus' broke a rib, I think. Doc Vi-lyn taped me up."

Eddie pushed past her into the kitchen. He dropped the fat pay envelope on the grimy tabletop where the muffled clatter of its landing spoke to them both of the certainty of another month's comfort. Breathless, he sat heavily into a chair. Not looking at her son, Edna shuffled past him to the stove.

"D'ya want me ta fry ya up a hamburger? It's way past lunch time."

"Nah. Gimme a glass a water."

She turned toward him, her eyes brightening a bit deep within the heavy folds of the lids.

"Sure ya wouldn't want just a bit a th' usual? Ah think ahm' gonna have just a nip."

When he didn't reply, she turned back toward the stove.

"Been waitin' a damn long time for ya."

Eddie squinted his eyes. He grabbed the envelope, turned his back on his mother, and sat forward over the table.

"Jus' gimme a glass a water. Ahm' gonna count my pay, an' then go see Ida."

Tearing one end from the envelope, Eddie spilled its contents onto the sticky wood of the table top. He placed the bills in low piles by denomination, then arranged the coin in a neat row of short columns of half dollars, quarters, dimes and nickels, then he sat back, contemplating his handiwork. Edna brought the glass of water, carefully setting it near the coins.

"Remember now, ma gets haf' a that," she said.

"If that's what ya want, ya kin' have it all," his voice rumbled darkly. "Ahm' goin' up ta lay down fer awhile. I don' feel so good."

He rose slowly and walked heavily from the room, leaving the glass of water untouched on the table.

The wind brought in the damp smells of the earth through the open window of his room. Eddie lay upon the bed in the blue-tinted afternoon light and pulled the wool blanket up to his chin. Warmth began to soothe the throbbing in his chest and brought with it the memory of a fragment of a long-past summer day. He must have been three or four years old, and he was with his father out in the backyard. He remembered his father rocking him. He'd held on, his arm trying to encircle the neck, his head resting against the sharp bone of the shoulder. He remembered the prickle of his father's long black mustache against the side of his face. Slowly they rocked together, and Eddie felt again another kind of warmth, deeper than that of the sun which had played over his skin; a warmth which had gone all the way to his heart. He'd gazed up to see the glimmer of sunlight through the gold and green canopy of trees.

Eddie found himself looking up at the bedroom's high ceiling whose crackled plaster reminded him of the tracery of pale blue veins across white skin. Somewhere he was conscious that he had entered the dream again. The Spring of

1945, three years ago now. He nodded in acknowledgement. The first that he had killed in combat was a girl. The force of the BAR that he'd carried had spun her about, torn off her coat and left her breast a tattered thing, its milky whiteness turning to the grey of plaster before his eyes. The ceiling became mottled storm clouds. Remains of bombed-out houses, their walls colored in angry shades of red and orange rose against a lowering sky. Open doorways and broken casements yawned blackly at him as Eddie made his way over the uneven pavement of narrow, lifeless streets. He gazed hungrily around each corner he passed, searching for the girl, for a glimpse of the doe-eyes, the long dark hair, and the mischievous smile playing across thin lips. When he couldn't find her, he searched for another, one less distinct, a jumbled memory of narrow shoulders, dark hair, a waxed moustache, the scent of lavender.

The fantastic necropolis faded into grey light. Eddie opened his eyes. The fragrance of baking bread, warm and sweet, rising from Maldutis Bakery across the alley filled the room. He remembered that it was Saturday afternoon, and they were baking for the churchgoers that would descend after Mass at St. Casimer's on Sunday morning. A few old women in dark sweaters and shawls, the occasional pensioned widower from the mills attired in a thin wool suit and dark fedora. Not a large batch, not like Monday mornings when the bread smell would permeate the predawn darkness. Eddie rolled carefully onto his side, drew his knees up toward his chin, and closed his eyes.

When he was just a little kid, and the weather was nice, his mother used to sit with him out on the porch facing the open doors of the squat blockhouse that held the bakery's ovens. The bakers would joke with them. They'd give him warm slices, and his mother would smile and whisper to the one who always walked over with the offering of fresh bread. Eddie saw again a later scene. He must have been fifteen or so and on his way late to school. He'd dashed off the porch and was heading toward those open doors when he saw one of the bakers, a broad fellow dressed in a dingy apron emerge from the oven house. His head was turned back toward the doorway.

"Goin' across th' way t' get my morning bone dance," he'd laughed, then turned and faced Eddie who was nearly upon him. The fellow stopped in his tracks and the smile vanished. His face turned red and he raised a dusty white hand to his cheek. Letting his eyes slip from Eddie's face, the baker stepped to one side and then abruptly turned and reentered the oven house. Eddie hurried on, afraid of looking back.

The big man awoke to the long shadows of the late afternoon. He rolled slowly onto his side, clenching his teeth against the agony rising in his chest. Standing, Eddie removed the dirty coveralls and grasped his only clean shirt and pants from the small chair next to the bed. The effort it took to lace up his shoes as he bent forward at the waist brought sweat to his forehead.

Downstairs in the kitchen he downed the glass of water Edna had set out for him earlier. She lay stretched across the sofa in the living room. In sleep her breast moved gently up and down with each shallow breath. On the low table before her the unstoppered, nearly empty bottle of Ballantine's Scotch stood tall among the crumpled cigarette packs and overflowing ashtrays. In the ambient grey light the fluted clear glass bottle looked like some ruined pillar in the midst of a miniature wasteland.

He grasped the handle of the front door and catching sight of the old wedding photograph, hesitated. His gaze focused on the jagged edge to the right of his mother's image. The photo had been ripped in half from top to bottom leaving only a blank expanse of yellowing mat board where the figure of his father had been. A scene of twenty years past rose before him: Edna pulling the photo from its frame, her eyes blazing and her hands working quickly while he had grasped at his father trying to restrain the narrow twisting shoulders with his arms, yelling, "I'm your son, I am your son!" Edna threw the wadded paper at the curtain over the front door's glass, making the lace shudder. His mother had turned then and run up the stairs, and Eddie heard a door slam shut. He remembered standing before that locked door, listening to the faint tinkling, knowing that the door would not be opened again until both bottle and glass on the small table next to what had been his parents' bed had long been empty. Sometime earlier from that bedroom Eddie'd heard the drone of his mother's voice rising and falling, the words indistinct, just at the edge of his understanding. Then he'd heard his father's voice, a harsh tenor rising above the hushed sounds of Edna's pleading.

"Aww, how th' hell do I know he's mine? How th' hell do I know what else yah ever been up to besides lappin' up th' booze?" The front door had slammed shut after Albert Geiger. It was the last time those curtains shook, the last time he'd seen his father. Eddie Geiger looked away from the photograph, and felt his face grow warm with shame. The pain deep within his chest was such that he shut his eyes and pulled his chin downward toward his breast. He waited a bit, then turned the handle of the door.

Held erect by the bands of tape about his chest, Eddie

slowly made his way down the alley. He headed west on Main Street toward Ida Payzak's flat in Slezak's block. The conflict of light and darkness still raged in the air, and a fretful wind tore about Eddie as he walked. He stopped, bracing himself against a streetlamp, coughed, waiting for the black cloud that rose at the edges of his sight to clear and then moved on. In the narrow foyer, he pressed the bell button twice, and not waiting for the buzzer on the door, inserted a key into the lock. Once inside the dark hallway, Eddie looked up to see Ida sitting on the last step before the second floor landing. Light from the single unshaded bulb hanging above her head softly shone on the thick blonde hair, broad forehead, and ample breasts. She stared down at him.

"I got hurt on th' damn tracks this mornin," he said in a soft rumble as he made his way up the stairs toward her.

"I know. Bad news travels fast."

Ida's voice resonated in the empty hallway. It seemed to hang in the air after the words had been uttered, reminding Eddie of the sweet nutlike aftertaste of sherry lingering on the tongue. He stopped, still below her, to catch his breath, and looked up at her eyes shining in the set, masklike face. Before the eyes of his memory rose a scene from long ago, when they were kids on the street and had spent an afternoon walking about and arguing. He could not remember the subject now, only the way her voice would giggle and guffaw each time she spoke in reply to him. And each time she'd objected to what he'd had to say, she'd punch at his shoulder or turn to face him and push both her hands flat against his chest. Suddenly when they'd reached her uncle's house, she'd run up on the porch and he'd followed her. All at once she turned toward him and took a step back.

"Get off th' porch," she'd said.

He remembered that he was set to argue with her, but then he looked at those large green eyes, brightly defiant. Her mouth was set as she stared at him.

"Go, on. Get off the porch," she'd repeated slowly in a quiet voice as though sharing a secret. And when he did, and with those green eyes staring into his, she'd reached down, slowly raising her skirt up to her thighs. She'd held him there for a long moment as his gaze had shifted from her eyes to the fascinating whiteness of her legs and back again to those eyes, bright with the triumph of desire. Then she'd let the skirt fall and run into the house. The sound of the screen door banging closed after her had felt like a slap to his face. In the dim hallway now those eyes shone with the same desire, but the gleam of triumph Eddie knew had long ago left them.

"Bernie was here awhile ago an' told me what happened."

"Ah get hurt an' he comes sniffin' around here," he said quietly.

Ida stood, and taking his hand, led the big man down the corridor. Inside her flat, she motioned him toward the table and turned, gently closing the door. Eddie slumped into a chair before the plate and glass she'd set for him. The effort of the walk and climbing the stairs had made him feel colder than when he'd awakened from his nap, and a heaviness settling in his chest had begun to strain against the tight bonds of the tape.

"Ahm' sorry, Ida."

She stood unmoving with her back to him. His gaze took in the yellow hair, proud shoulders, gentle curve of upper back, soft outline of hips and thighs. The comfort he knew was his to find there pulled at his loins but not at his heart.

Ida turned to face him. She held herself erect, leaning

back against the stove, her arms crossed beneath her breasts.

"Bernie told me how it happened."

Her wide eyes, moistened with a thin film of tears, searched his face.

"You know I don't care for him. But I just can't live with, or bury, a drunk," she said, the desperation in her voice undercutting the ultimatum.

For an instant he felt his heart reach out, but then dark, doe-eyes and a thin mischievous smile stirred in his memory. He sat still at the table, avoiding Ida's stare. A sense of loss crept upon him. It was as though the part of him that cared about the living and the dead had been torn away. He sat in numbed silence.

Ida stirred herself, took a pot from the stove and brought it to the table, setting it before him. Eddie ate a bit in silence, then stopped and raised his head to look at her. She came and sat opposite him.

"Ah ain't th' best person in th' world. Ah know that. Ah hurt people. There're things Ah done. Yuh know that, Ida."

He stopped and stared down at the half-empty plate, conscious of the fretful sound of the wind tearing at the loose casement of the kitchen window, the play of light and shadow coursing through the room. When he spoke again, it was with surrender to the noise and light which raged outside, to the agony abiding in his chest and in his memory, to the green eyes insistent upon him.

"Ah can't fergit, that's all."

Ida heard the emptiness that neither food nor words could fill, reached across the table and took one of his hands, cradling it in both of hers. He stood, and she led him to her bed where they lay down next to each other.

"My chest hurts s'bad, Ah can't do nuthin," he said.

She brought his hand to her lips.

“We don’ have ta do nuthin’,” she whispered.

As the shadows of dusk crept over them, the wind seemed to subside, its sound reduced to a faint scratching at the window pane. Eddie heard the gentle cadence of Ida’s breath. He opened his eyes and started to turn, seeking her warmth against the chill of the evening falling quickly about him.

The shock of the gut-punch he’d received that morning came again. This time he was held suspended. Numbness rose from his chest outward to his arms and jaw and flowed down his legs. From the edges of his vision a soft darkness rushed upon him.

Bernie At The Atlas

Bernie Andrulis slowly pushed his way through the noontime crowd outside the Adirondack Busline's waiting room. Out of habit his eyes searched the passersby for detail that might be memorable. It could be anything, a furrowed brow, the tense set of jaw or lips, a stumbling, uncertain gait, that would speak of an inner life he'd not yet been able to imagine. But today the throng seemed made up of those whose closed faces and determined steps suggested that the bus station was only a wearisome obstacle to be endured on the way to somewhere else. As he passed Slezak's tenement the crowd thinned a bit, and Bernie's attention switched focus. He stopped and looked up at the front of the apartment building. The windows on all five floors were shut and curtained against the bright sun. Next door the rank growth of weeds in the empty lot bordering St.Casimer's Church provided a luxuriant green contrast to the burnt rust color of Slezak's block. Bernie noted the profusion of yellow dandelions standing tall and brilliant above the darker greens of crab grass and young burdock. There was no doubt now that the earth had awakened to the touch of the June sun. The vegetation, fecund and grasping, had run riot over the grey rubble of winter.

Bernie quickened his step, passing the darkly tinted glass front of Soltys' Funeral Chapel. Ahead, the rest of the street was deserted, quiet in the still air. At the corner of East Main and Schuyler sat the Atlas Hotel and Tavern, and Bernie turned and strode through the open door. The place looked as though it had just been deserted by its revelers. Stools and tables were scattered about the room, empty schooners littered the bar and the red globe lights on either side of the mirrored wall behind the tiers of bottles flickered weakly in the mid-day brightness. A lone patron at the far end of the bar sat hunched forward. At Bernie's approach the slight figure turned slowly round, revealing the narrow almost chinless face of Colley McIntyre. Bernie watched as the young man's eyes went wide in recognition, his mouth opening in a sudden oval as though he were gasping for air, then resolved itself into a lopsided smile.

"Heyy, Bernie, how th' hell are yeh?" Colley's eyes gleamed with the excited camaraderie of booze.

Bernie snorted in reply lifting his gaze to the grimy tin ceiling. Colley sensed the air of a man who had just seen something dirty and wearily predictable, like maybe a small pile of dog shit in the street that had to be stepped around, so he forged ahead breathlessly.

"Hey. Old Man Rakstis ain't so good today, so I came in to lend a hand." His eyes moved away from Bernie, taking in the room. "I'm just lendin' a hand to tidy up a bit, get ready for later. Yeh know, Saturday night's always a big night."

Bernie lowered his gaze from the patterns of fruits and leaves embossed across the ceiling and held Colley with his eyes.

"Takin' yer pay in booze before th' work's done, uh?"

The unblinking eyes set above the high cheekbones and beaklike nose took Colley's measure, and Colley felt that he was being held in the stare of some sort of predator.

"Aw, what th' hell, I'm just havin' a nip. Yuh want one? Yuh can always have a nip, can't yuh? Take th'edge off th' afternoon," Colley offered quietly. He shook his head slightly from side to side and seemed to be studying the motes of dust dancing in the beams of bright light that slanted through the large windows facing East Main.

"Damn kids get tuh me by th' end of th' week. So's I need a little diversion come th' weekend. So what, who th' hell's it hurt?" he shrugged, not wanting to challenge Bernie.

"Who th' hell says it hurts anybody? Yuh need booze, yuh need booze, that's all." Bernie tossed back.

Colley sat silent in reply. His eyes sought the floor. Looking down on him, Bernie saw that his gaze had turned inward, maybe making him the captive of a memory farther back than just last week's encounters with his indifferent charges at the local high school.

Bernie turned away and started toward the hotel desk at the back of the bar room. His boots caught a sticky patch on the floor, and he looked over to see his reflection gliding across the bar mirror's wavy surface. The mottled pinks and whites of his face and the amber of his beard faded as the image passed through a large grey blotch where the silver had dropped away from the back of the glass. For an instant he wondered where he was or even if he was at all. The image of a dying deer he'd seen on the railroad tracks suddenly forced its way into his memory. The animal hadn't cleared the rails fast enough and its back had been clipped by a passing express. He saw the deer's rolling eyes wide with the darkness of approaching death, its red mouth gaping, the head tossing as it lay across the ballast at the trackside. He thought of Colley. You get too close to things you can't control and they'll do you no good at all. Forever.

Old Jack Rakstis the day manager was asleep in the shadows behind the reception desk near the stairs. He sat with his head thrown far back in the chair, the yellow skin of his skull-face drawn tight over the bone, the dark gape of mouth outlined by thin blue lips. A harsh, wet gurgle rose from his throat, and Bernie knew again where he was and what that sound meant. Every day when the old man fell asleep behind the counter, the Atlas was treated to the same swan song, the only gift Rakstis had gotten from forty years spent in the Bigelow-Sanford dye house. Another example of embracing something you couldn't control, thought Bernie, as he made his way up the creaking stairs to the second floor landing. There the noise of a door slamming somewhere down the hall made him pause, for he feared it the sound of many doors closing against him in the only place that he could now call home.

Bernie forced himself toward the faint halo of light outlining the door to his rooms. Over the years the thin wood had warped away from the jamb. He fished the key from the pocket of his overalls and grasped the dented knob clammy with the grease of numberless fingers. There was a faint click and the door swung inward of its own accord.

The room was awash in a blaze of light streaming through the large curtain-less window in the far wall. Bernie struggled out of his overalls and threw them on the crumpled mass of grey sheets piled at the foot of the narrow bed. He turned to avoid the merciless glare, his gaze passing quickly over the kitchen alcove where pots, dishes, and glassware lay scattered about the sink and stove top. Farther over, beyond the small wooden icebox, the door to his tiny windowless bathroom stood ajar. That private bath made his room the most expensive one the Atlas offered. With a railroad man's pay he'd be damned if he'd share a craphouse with the rummies and worn out whores who regularly called the Atlas home. Well, it was his home now too, and he'd goddamned make the best of it, even though the light in the place was all wrong, too intense because it came from the south and west.

Bernie closed the door and faced the wall opposite the window. The tall-legged clerk's desk, a small easel fastened to its top, was tucked into a corner. Next to the desk a stand held open cigar boxes filled with pieces of charcoal and pastel spread over a layer of rice. Among the boxes were scattered tubes of artist's paint and brushes. Bernie's gaze rose to the wall. Tacked to the dark green plaster was a colored photo of Goya's The Naked Maja neatly scissored from a book. Around the photo were placed red chalk drawings of nudes, seated and standing, their faces and bodies modeled in such striking detail of highlight and shadow that the flesh of each figure suggested the personality of an individual man or woman. Out beyond the nudes were tacked a few smaller landscapes of the Mohawk Valley whose greens and golds were so heavily rendered the colors seemed to pulse in the bright light. Bernie squinted and the wall appeared bejeweled with the warm glow of a large diamond circled by the luscious colors of smaller gems. He looked again at each of the figure studies and waited. Slowly the fear and anger left him. He grew calm in the certainty that in those drawings he could see others as they really were, in the cast of their eyes, the set of their mouths, the way they walked or sat in repose. When he transferred those faces and bodies to paper he knew he bore witness to the grand dreams and narrow terrors that haunted the lives of others. They were the only true things, hard and fast and true forever.

Bernie turned and gazed out of the small window above the kitchen sink. Across the lot next to St. Casimer's he could see where Forbes Street curved down towards East Main, and his eyes were drawn to a white house in the middle of the block. He could make out the delicately cut wooden gingerbread and ornately fluted railings of the porches that wrapped around the front of the place. Even at this distance he could also see the expanses of grey wood exposed by the peeling paint. The windows on the second floor were uncurtained black rectangles cut into the clapboard, and Bernie, as he raised his hands to wipe the grime of the morning's labor from around his eyes, looked again into one of those bedrooms shadowed in the late winter dawn.

He heard the rush of sleet pattering against the window glass above his head, and breathed again the musky scent of the woman whose warm flesh clung soft against him. Her dark eyes opened slowly to watch his face while her arms circled his neck. Her legs slick and moist as the bodies of eels might be, sought to twine themselves about his own. He labored to draw breath in the warm, cloying air, turned away from her grasp, and lay still upon his back.

"He'll be gettin' up soon," he'd offered by way of apology.

"Jesus Christ, lover, we made enough noise most a'th' night; he probably ain't had any time ta' sleep anyway. C'mon, baby, just one more for Valentine's Day." She'd laughed softly, her voice rich with anticipation and promise.

Bernie rolled from under the heavy quilt and sat up, hunched at the edge of the bed. After a moment he'd felt the mattress shift as it gave up the burden of his partner's weight. He'd turned to watch her as she switched on the ceiling bulb and stood at the dresser mirror, her back to him. Slowly she'd begun combing out the matted kinks of her long black hair. She'd finished, turned to stare at him, cocking her head to one side, spreading her arms away from her body, shifting one leg slightly forward holding that pose a moment. Her eager dark eyes had appraised him.

"How about some more of this?" she murmured smiling.

Bernie assessed her nakedness. The pendulous pear-shaped breasts with their dark umber aureoles and nipples thrusting downward, a belly white and hips as full as Botticelli's Venus, the triangle of hair so dark it shone blueblack in the yellow of the overhead light. Millie Lipari was a madonna of the flesh.

He'd recalled the night's image of Millie in the dim light, eyes shut, offering herself without shame or reservation. At first he drove against her in maddening desire, and when she responded with the insistent clasp of her flesh, he'd grown fearful and then angry. Her desperate embrace told him she would surround and possess him. He would be hers. He would be nothing.

"You want me to go, Bernie?"

"If ya want, Millie." He'd looked away. "Ya know how th' old man'll get if he catches on … ta what's goin' on …." His voice trailed off. He'd stared intently out the window at the growing brightness of dawn.

"Oh, baby, you're th' only one who don't know what's goin' on!" she'd spat back.

He'd heard the soft, quick rustle of Millie dressing behind him. She sat abruptly down on the mattress so that the springs rattled noisily. Then the floor shook as she'd stomped her feet into the boots. Bernie had turned to see her struggling into her coat. She'd looked at him boldly, her chin thrust forward as if daring him to break the night's promise. Then her dark eyes had begun to fill with tears, she'd reached a hand up to smooth her hair and shook her head as if to cast aside a troublesome memory. He'd led her along the dimly lit hallway past the thin bar of light glowing beneath the closed door of his father's room. They'd slipped quietly down the stairs, and at the front door Millie had turned to look at him with angry, guarded eyes. He'd remained silent, turning the key in the lock, and Millie had walked off in the grey morning toward her flat in Slezak's block. When Bernie had closed the door, he'd turned to see his father standing just a pace behind him.

The growing heat of the early afternoon flooding into his room made it impossible for Bernie to sustain the memory. The layer of grime clung heavily to his face and neck. The sour odor of sweat hung about him. He entered the small bathroom, slowly shed his clothes, and climbed into the grey claw-footed tub. As he sat before the opened faucets waiting for the tepid water to rise around him, his gaze roamed over the narrow line of pale blue tiles running round the circumference of the room halfway between floor and ceiling. The color reminded him of his father's eyes. Of a sudden he was back to that grey February morning and Vitty Andrulis was staring up at him with those eyes that seemed too large for the round face.

"*Kekse*. Don't bring your whore into my house." Vitty had said quietly, the baleful blue eyes fixed on his son.

"It's my house too." Bernie had shot back, wanting to crush the old man beneath the force of his words, but the sound of his voice had been high and tinny.

"Not no more. Not no more it ain't. Get the hell out with your whore. Get the hell out… the hell … out!" The voice reverberated down the halls of memory, its tone that of a feudal lord who'd always looked out on the world with an absolute faith in his own judgment. Bernie reflected on how different he and the old man had looked. Vitty, short, barrel-chested and bull-necked whose son could not remember his father ever having even a wisp of hair on his head or the hint of beard across his cheek. And Bernie, tall, raw-boned, with a mane of unruly red-blond hair and a pig's bristle goatee the color of amber. He'd gotten his looks from his tall red-haired mother, gaunt with the burden of a bad heart, and dead at her only son's birth. At least that's what his much older sisters had always said. The baloney twins Vitty had called them. Short, as rotund as their father, and driven off long ago by the old man's brutal certainty. No, he didn't look like the old man, but Bernie knew he was Vitty's son in the way he looked at the world. There are no greys. Only black and white and judgments are forever.

Time passed and the bath water cooled. Bernie stood, stepped from the tub and drew the grey towel about his waist. The threadbare material felt cool and damp about his skin and he remembered the coldness of his father's hands, folded one upon the other across the once-proud chest sunken to fit the narrow confines of the coffin.

"He went quick." Bernie recalled Jack Rakstis' throaty rasp over the phone line on that other Saturday morning a month after he'd been thrown out of the house. "Yeah, he went quick. Just fell on the sidewalk outside the waiting room. Don't know if he was gonna take a bus or what the hell he was doin' down there. They said he was dead when he hit th' ground."

There were few mourners at Soltys'. His sisters, a couple of the old man's cronies from the American Lithuanian Club, and Father Dichavicius from St. Casimer's. Millie hadn't come. He'd not seen her since that February morning, although once the weather had turned warm, he'd looked for her every time he'd passed Slezak's block on his way back to the Atlas from work.

Bernie stood still letting the warm air dry his skin. There were no sounds from the street or from any of the other rooms in the Atlas. After a while, he stepped beyond the door of the bath into the larger room where the weight of the silence and the light bore down unremittingly upon him. His eyes sought the wall that held his drawings. In the painful glare they seemed just formless blobs of color. Bernie took a quick step forward and tried to look out of the small kitchen window, but the angle of the sun across the dirty glass made it impossible to see his father's house. He stood still, his mind racing with thoughts of Millie and the old man. As the one had cast him away, so too had he cast away the other. The bright air began to suffocate him, and when he tried to draw a breath the taste of abandonment lay bitter in his mouth. He must leave the Atlas, make his way over to Slezak's. Downstairs he would no doubt pass the sleeping Rakstis and Colley who by now was sure to be comatose on the bar. Bernie dressed quickly and descending the stairs heard voices mixed with what sounded like the tinkling of glass.

The reception desk was deserted. Bernie made his way to the barroom where the air was coolish. The front door had been closed, and the air conditioner in the transom above gave off a low hum. Tables had been spaced in even rows, and with a quick step Jack Rakstis was pushing chairs across the newly mopped floor. Bernie noticed that his face had lost its yellow pallor. Jack's cheeks were flushed a bright pink. Indifferent to Bernie's prescence, he did not look up as the gandy dancer passed. Over at the bar, Colley was busy with a soapy rag. He too was silent, and as Bernie stared at him, Colley looked up with steady eyes. Then he went back to scrubbing down the bar. Out in the street Bernie raised a hand to shade his brow. The dazzling sunlight made it painful for him to look toward the west where Slezak's block lay waiting, and with uncertain step, Bernie stumbled ahead into a world he could no longer imagine.

Amsterdam

Have a
Pepsi
Giuffre's
Schell's
PHARMACY
HOTEL
TAVERN

HOTEL
TAVERN
SCHELL'S
PHARMACY
PRESCRIPTIONS

Jack

My grandfather Jack is a mystery to me. Few are the actual recollections I have of him, even though we shared the same house for the last declining decade of his life. Yet those sparse memories are the most vivid of my childhood. I see Jack struggling to rise from his chair near the downstairs front door. I hear the heavy footfalls of his wide-stanced gait as he lumbers toward the unheated bedroom behind my grandmother's kitchen. In my memory the echoes of his angry curses still sound in long-vanished rooms.

Where my grandfather's anger came from I do not know with certainty. Years after his death my mother told me that her father-in-law had been very wild as a youth, and that his marriage to my grandmother, a woman several years his senior, had been an effort by the family to tame Jack's youthful ferocity. But when my mother told me this her own memory had been clouded by ninety years of living, nearly thirty of which had been spent at war with her mother-in-law. So time and the emptiness that comes with having outlasted one's enemies may have clouded her recollection.

I do know that from his early youth Jack had been a real toper. Indeed, at his wake I remember old Tighe, a drinking buddy from the American Lithuanian Club, telling the story of Jack's once dipping into jars of new elderberry wine my great grandmother had put up in her cellar.

"Jesus," says Tighe in a breathless whisper, his eyes wide and rheumy with remembered excitement and new drink, "When he was just a little guy even, th' kid goes down there half loaded with some farmers' matches an' a bit a candle an' tries to re-seal th' bottles so's his ma won't catch on. But he don't know that there's air in 'em jars when he melts the wax or whatever. Pretty soon, they're blowin' up underneath th' old lady's bedroom in th' middle of th' night! Then she's scared and won't go down there fer days in case a jar explodes when she gets close to it. An' yah know, his ma never did find out what made them jars explode." The constant tremor that moves Tighe's pig-pink head from side to side increases in amplitude.

"Damn me, if he was never that lucky again in his whole life!"

Huddling over Tighe, my father and his younger brother share a quiet chuckle well out of earshot of my grandmother and aunt crying at the bier.

They wept for three days of the wake, and their tears flowed even faster at the graveside than the dark torrents of November rain. Then all the crying stopped. Jack's bed and meager wardrobe were dispatched to the Salvation Army, and his name was never again mentioned in the house that three generations of our family shared.

And yet for me Jack is more than just an angry alcoholic, for if we care to acknowledge it, experience teaches that others close to us defy the simple labels. We share with them the web of hopes and fears that befuddle our own hearts. For us they can never be just a son, just a mother, just a drunk.

My earliest memory of Jack dates to when I was five or six. In a kitchen redolent with the salty sweet aroma of roasting beef, my younger cousin and I are ushered to the table, our chins close above its dented grease-green metal edge. An important mystery of the adult world is about to be revealed. Jack, resplendent in sleeveless undershirt, sits close at the head of the table, his face dominated by a nose as massive and angular as the head of a splitter's maul. The jaw line is broad enough to complement that nose and makes his head look as though it were a wedge struck haphazardly from a larger piece of granite. Up close I can discern the pink and grey patina of his weathered neck and cheeks. Before him is a plate heaped with steaming beef fat. Against the crackles spread like spider webs across the porcelain glaze the rinds bubble dark brown, their pearly inner surfaces glistening in all the colors of the rainbow. Great slabs of yellow cheese rim the edge of the platter.

"Here, c'mon, eat this. It'll make men outta yah!"

My cousin suddenly clamps his mouth shut and starts to whimper, but I am older and shrug off the enticement of his tears. I will not cry and manage a lung full of air sour with the odors of whiskey and stale sweat before the quivering forkful is shoved against my lips. I bite down hard, as I imagine a man would, chew a bit and swallow. But there is no mystery. There is only the insipid taste of gristle. I want no more. I try the cheese, but its sharpness stings my tongue and my eyes tear. I back away from the table as Jack turns from me, silent, dismissive. It is as though we both understand that I have not measured up to a man's world, and I am angry at myself and at Jack for he has shown me that I am too soft and gentle yet and cannot see the beauty of strong and savage things.

It is the last year of Jack's life. March rain turns a long grey twilight blue-black as I watch wind-driven water ripple against the thin panes of the bay window. I fancy myself grown now, capable of knowing Jack. At my back, the warm kitchen fills with the bustle and chirp of my grandmother and aunt as they move about preparing supper. Yet beneath the comforting aromas of the warming meal lurks the sharp odor of pine bleach. It is a hint to my youthful understanding that what is not approved must be ruthlessly scoured away. Still my heart is buoyed when Jack appears at the front door, drenched and sober from the road. With heavy step he moves past me without a glance. I wait, listen cautiously, hopefully, but in the kitchen, recriminations begin. The floors are wet, the voice too loud, the demand for dinner too early and too often made.

"Shh, shhh, the boy'll hear."

I see Jack, at bay, turning to his wife and daughter, crying with a heart that must speak loudly and at once,

"So what if he does! Let him know what he's in for too … someday!"

"Now look, you! You've made him cry!"

The women's angry shrieks surpass Jack's sputtering thunder. Again and again their sharply scolding voices harry him; to me he seems a dying bull tormented by the sword. The door to his unheated bedroom behind the kitchen stove slams shut, and I am left alone staring at my reflection in the dark window glass.

Sunday night. In celebration of St. Patrick, Jack's been gone two days. Every light in the house is lit, and I am at my accustomed space on the overstuffed sofa, my feet not quite reaching the floor. The women move from room to room whispering words hard-edged with fear.

"Oh, he's over at Kavanaugh's, sleepin' it off, probably."

"Tom Kehoe saw 'im at the ALC Saturday afternoon. Said he was in no shape to come home. Said he probably was afraid to anyway."

In the brightness the familiar living room has become cavernous, its dusty walls and stained ceiling violently beaten back. Car brakes squeal and light flashes across the window curtains' deep folds making them appear like thick white bars set against the black night. Men's voices rumble cautiously as their footsteps shake the porch. The knob rattles a bit, turns slowly, then the door swings wide revealing Jack, white-faced, slack-jawed, with outstretched hands grasping the jamb. He lifts one shaking foot onto the threshold and rises, braced from behind by old Tighe and the cabdriver. Struggling, they lower him deep into the flattened cushion of his chair just inside the door. Jack raises his elbows high onto the armrests so that his outstretched forearms are nearly on a level with his chin. Then his head droops forward. Old Tighe straightens up. With an apologetic grimace he offers,

"Had a bit much at the ALC, he did."

Carefully watching the carpet Tighe pivots about and makes for the open door. The cabdriver follows him, and they vanish into the night.

Jack sits Lincolnesque in a stupor until the call to supper comes. My father and uncle approach, gently pull him upright. They try to move him away from the chair, but his weight is too much for them. All three are borne down toward the tray table. In slow motion I see Jack sit down upon the bottom tray and hear the sharp crack of its cut lace wooden edge breaking off. The furies in the kitchen who've been silent until now are roused.

"Oh, look what he's done! My mother's table!"

"Oh, whatever he touches he turns to rubbish."

"You'll see! You'll get that fixed. You'll have Andrulis do it. Dirty drunken old man, you'll pay for this!"

The warm days of summer arrive. In the few months following his retirement from the road, Jack has become for me a worrisome presence lurking about the neighborhood. At any moment of the late afternoon he's liable to appear, silent, wooden-faced, ham-fisted, his cane tapping fitfully on the pavement as he makes his way home from the ALC. I am always on the lookout. When I catch sight of him, I escape to my bedroom, there to fear the slow staccato of his step along the porch, the crash of the front door slamming shut, the tempest from which no one in the house can find shelter. Even when he is not at home, I feel the weight of his heavy step and thunderous voice. As the days advance, my heart grows angry at the burden.

When the last storm comes, it is strangely brief. A few curses deep and low are answered by higher-pitched accusations fleeting as the quick rap of hail against a window pane. I wait in the long silence that follows until the rank smoke of Jacks' soiled trousers slowly burning in the backyard fireplace finally drives me from the house.

That silence lasts into late November. The long shadows of a Sunday afternoon steal quietly across cold gray pavement when the screaming of women explodes in the hallway. Then comes the stumbling rush down the stairs, the hurried phone call and the siren song diminishing as it nears our house. Hidden behind a chair shoved against an upstairs window, I hear the footfalls of firemen thundering on the porch below. Later, in the living room downstairs, I want to hide again. But there is no sanctuary large enough now to shelter me behind the sofa or beneath the bay window. I watch as Jack's shroud-covered body, strapped to a board, is levered erect from the undertaker’s gurney and carried through the narrow doorway into the night.

Mary

On the buffet two framed sepia photographs stand side by side against the large decanter. Records not of what has been done, but of what has been lost. Objects that haunt the imagination, that whet the desire to fathom the history of a family I arrived too late to know. Aunt Mary, my mother Agnes' oldest sister. First born, and therefore solely deserving of the photographic record of his daughter that an immigrant carpenter sacrificed to provide. The year of one portrait is 1921, the year of her marriage. The husband-to-be was Albert Flaherty, a hard-drinking blonde-haired Irish boy from the north end of Albany, New York. The only bridesmaid, Edna Hogan, consumptive, a gaunt and bony farm girl from Hoosick Falls. But these are details that other memories intrude, for in the portrait Mary stands in three-quarter profile, alone. Her dark brown hair is bobbed and shines with brilliantine. There is a look of gentle confidence about the eyes. Her cheek is full and smooth, the lips set in a self-reliant pout with chin raised jauntily to the world. The heavy silver bangle earring just touches a frilly boa draped over the dark velvet figure of her appliqué coat.

The other picture is what is left of a wedding photo torn in half. The jagged edge of the paper blazes like lightening against the darkened mat. It speaks silently in that special language of broken things. Mary and Edna wear veils and hold bouquets of white flowers. The women stare apprehensively at the camera as if shocked by the sudden absence of Albert and his anonymous groomsman. Albert's actual departure would come a bit later, perhaps a result of the unwanted arrival of a son, or just the ennui that is the certain peril of young romance.

In the gloom of the late summer dusk an apparition of dried hair, withered cheeks, and searching eyes draws near to me.

"Al, Al, … yuh finally come back!"

Bewildered, embarrassed, I offer quietly,

"No, no. It's me … it's Danny."

"Eddie. Eddie. Is that you?" her voice rises in fretful hope that the boy who stands before her might be the little one lost so many years before. The heavy scent of scotch surrounds me. I draw back a pace or two.

"No. No. It's me. Dan."

The figure moves a bit from side to side, silently staring.

"It's me. It's Dan. Agnes' boy. Agnes' boy," I say again and again into a silence that only forty years of abandonment and one dead son can bring.

Albert's Story

Albert Geiger moves cautiously in the dim light. He does not want to risk knocking into any of the chairs stacked, seat-side down, onto the small tables. A racket down here might wake his wife Edna upstairs long before it is necessary for her to be in the kitchen. Reaching the front of the lunchroom, Albert grasps the clammy edge of the oilcloth shade and gives a gentle tug, then stands staring out the large window, watching as shadows mottle the cobblestones of the silent street.

East Main is deserted, and as time passes Albert watches the grey of night slowly change to the pale blue of dawn. After the sun breaks above the rooftops, points of gold begin to glint along the dull silver ribbons of the trolley tracks that run up the middle of the pavement. Across the street old Lithuanian women start to gather on the sidewalk in front of St. Casimir's Church. Their bodies are block-like, draped in long dark coats, and their heads, covered by colorless scarves, are bent towards one another. Each has a hand raised to her lips.

They're sharing secrets, thinks Albert. Each is fortunate to be sharing a secret with her sister. They're waiting too. Every morning they wait for the church to be unlocked from the inside. Soon, the heavy double doors break apart and old Baltch the janitor sticks his white-maned head out, nodding towards the small congregation gathered for early Mass. The women file in one after the other, the last closing the door against the growing brightness of the street. Albert turns away, reflecting with small satisfaction that at least some things can be relied upon, and walks over to raise the four shades that cover the smaller windows fronting Eagle Street. The restaurant has a good corner location near the carpet mills farther down the East End. Albert thinks back to 1928 when he'd first opened. Ten years, now. He hadn't had the money for a sign then, but he did pay extra to have Guiffre letter "Geiger's Lunchroom" in fancy gold script across all the windows, so no matter what direction you came from, you knew he was right here, convenient, indispensible. Just stop in for a quick bite and you're on your way.

In those early days the lunchroom had done well. Mohawk'd had a third shift and they used to get a good breakfast crowd. Mostly skeiners, weavers, and the night watchmen. There were the rougher bunch from receiving and shipping, too. Guys who'd worked most of the night getting the bales of wool and jute off-loaded and the finished carpets rolled and packed into the cars on the New York Central siding. He'd always gotten along with them. He remembers how they'd kid him about his mustache, for the most distinguishing mark of Albert Geiger's appearance is the luxuriant black handlebar that overspreads his upper lip and whose points, sharply waxed, reach half way across his broad, pale cheeks.

"Hey, how's that pussy tickler, this mornin'', eh?" one old skeiner would always whisper after he'd hopped up onto a counter stool, motioning at Albert to lean in close to him. The odor of sweat and dago wine on the old guy's breath filled Albert's nostrils. Nodding, he'd stare back at the millhand.

"Uh, huh," he'd say.

Then he'd whisper so's Edna wouldn't hear,

"An when's th' last time you had a taste?" The guy's cronies would laugh softy and shake their heads. Yeah, always the same greeting, the same jokes. Those guys had squared themselves with their limitations, laboring in darkness and looking forward only to a fitful sleep in the hard light of day. Edna could handle them too. She'd flash those beautiful bold eyes at a comment or a look that went too far, and the guys would look away uneasily. No one of them ever made another comment or leered at her a second time.

Albert hears the sounds of Edna fussing about the narrow galley kitchen that runs behind a low wall in back of the counter. It holds the grill, a large icebox, and the butcher block, a three foot wide slab of elm set into an old cheese wheel that he'd had the good fortune to get when McClumpha's grocery went under. At the far end of the galley is the small toilet, just a sink and bowl, where their son Eddie is busy primping his hair for school.

"C'mon, c'mon," Albert hears Edna badgering as she raps at the door to the john.

"Yuh almost done? Yuh gotta get goin'. It's a walk to Division Street."

Albert moves back toward Edna just as Eddie emerges from the small bathroom.

"Aw, ma, why can't I just stay at home 'til it's time tuh git tuh school? Division ain't that far. Why can't I just take care of myself upstairs in the morning now?"

He looks pleadingly at Albert.

"Cause I need yuh down here where I can keep an eye on yuh, instead of havin' yuh sneakin' about where I don't know where yuh are. Yer gettin' little too big fer yerself lately!"

Edna stands glaring at Eddie, her mouth set and her chin thrust forward. Al watches the boy's soft brown eyes trying to avoid his mother's belligerent stare. At thirteen he's already more than a head taller than his parents and broader in the shoulders than his father. Eddie moves off quietly toward the front door. Albert grabs the push broom, turns and follows him. Out on the sidewalk he puts a hand on his son's shoulder, and as the boy turns to him, slips a nickel into his hand. Albert looks into Eddie's eyes for a long moment and the image of the old women sharing secrets in front of St. Casimir's flashes across his memory.

"Go wan," Albert finally says, "don't worry about it."

Eddie ducks his head low, turns and starts west toward Division Street.

Albert bends over the broom. He starts sweeping at the sidewalk with short jabs. After a bit he looks up trying to catch a last glimpse of his son retreating in the distance, but Eddie's disappeared and Albert sees Adonis Pelagiaone stacking crates of fruits and vegetables on the sidewalk in front of his father's market several doors past the corner of Eagle and East Main. He feels his heart quicken a bit as he stops sweeping and straightens up watching the unmarried grocery clerk.

Cock of the walk, Albert thinks. Comes swaggering into the lunchroom every day now even though Pelagiaone Market does a good business of its own in cold cuts and bread.

"Call me Donny, Donny Piccollo. What th' hell, even I got trouble sayin' the family name. Besides, that's all old country stuff, anyway."

Donny looks in Albert's direction. His dark hair is a tight mass of blue -black curls. After a second or so, he flashes a broad, square-jawed smile, waving and nodding. Then he's back to arranging the bushels and sacks, his back and thighs bulging against the tight fitting white shirt and dark pants while the muscles of his forearms below the rolled sleeves are sharp in the pale light of the morning sun.

The lunch crowd starts to trickle in around eleven-thirty. The office help from the lower mill are first. Portly middle-aged men in wool suits with vests, the wide brims of their soft-looking fedoras are turned down, shadowing their pasty faces. In groups of two or three they seek tables at the back of the place. Then come the younger girls from the offices chattering and giggling. They always take the tables closer to the counter. Right after the noon whistle blows, the mill hands barge through the door, wanting to fill their half hour at the counter with as much food as they can.

Albert tends the counter while Edna handles the tables. They both run the grill and the register to cash people out. Amid the din, Albert looks over at Edna as she moves about. Her profile still captivates him. The bobbed black hair frames a face so white it seems to glow in the blue haze of cigarette smoke that hangs in the air. The longish nose and prominent cheekbones seem to make her red lips fuller and more pronounced. A slight smile moves across those lips as she listens to the banter of the diners giving their orders.

Albert remembers the day he first saw her in the GE cafeteria in Schenectady. She sat at a table near the floor to ceiling windows that let in a cascade of light from Erie Boulevard. Albert remembers: the bluish white light of the dining hall and the image of that girl sitting at a table near the door, one leg crossed over the other, swinging girlishly. Edna wore a white blouse and dark skirt tight at the hips, but fuller below the knee. She glanced about as though lost or maybe just on the lookout for someone she'd been expecting. Her long black hair gleamed in silver highlights every time she turned her head. Suddenly it seemed to Albert that she became conscious of his gaze, and turned her profile. Then she stared directly at him. He looked away quickly, but then stole a glance. Albert remembers doing that three times and then knowing that he'd never be able to look away again.

At first he thought she might be an executive secretary for one of the bigwigs, and lost heart of ever talking to her. Then he found out that she was a runner for the mail room and that had given him the confidence to say hello to her. She'd told him that her name was Edna Dailey and had arched her eyebrows when he said he was a cook in the company cafeteria. But then she'd let him treat her to lunch every day during his break. When he showed up that first time at her cramped flat in Slezaks' block on East Main, he discovered that her real name was Dailide, and that her parents were Lithuanians who couldn't speak a word of English. She'd started to apologize but then burst forth with a breathless speech about her dreams of escaping the narrow life of an immigrant's daughter. He'd listened, fascinated. Her desire for better prospects awoke in him a long unspoken dream for a restaurant of his own. Edna's dark eyes spoke the secrets of her heart and flashed a bold defiance at the dimly lit kitchen where she and Albert had sat at the heavy, unwrought wooden table. Her mother and father had crouched in the background, smiling and nodding. They could not understand their daughter's words but they knew all too well the passion that possessed her. Later, when Albert had begun to reach out and caress her, Edna had suddenly drawn close, cupped his face in her hands and looked steadily into his eyes.

"It's no wallflower you're getting." Her voice was low and sensuous, yet more challenge than confession. That voice, her dark hair, the flush of her face as she held him were overwhelming.

"It's none I want."

The words had escaped him unawares, and in an instant Albert knew that she was the stronger. It was a secret he could share with no one. To this day he did not know if Edna understood or even cared about the hold she had on him.

The flood of memory stops when Albert sees Donny Piccollo striding through the door. He pauses just inside, surveying the lunchroom. Albert looks for Edna and sees her at one of the tables. She raises her head, the smile still on her lips, and looks directly at Donny. Piccollo lifts his chin in her direction. Albert sees Edna's gaze follow Donny as he moves toward the counter where every stool is taken. The Greek places his hands on the shoulders of two dye house workers and wedges himself between them.

"Hey, Al, I kin see that yer real busy, but kin yah get me a coupla yer ham specials tah go? I kin wait." Donny smiles, nods and winks as though he's sharing a secret with his best friend. Albert lets his eyes slip from Donny's face. His gaze runs along the counter, his lips twist themselves into an expression halfway between a grimace and a grin.

"What's a matter, Adonis, yer cold cuts go bad?"

"Hey, hey, it's Donny...remember? Nah, it's just yah got th' best hot stuff in th' East End, yuh know? I can't deny myself now, can I?"

The Greek turns to Tom Cuddy, the foreman of the dye house who sits on the stool to his left. His grin broadens and he inhales deeply in a self-satisfied way. Cuddy doesn't look up from his plate, and for an instant the din of the lunchroom grows silent in Albert's ears. He's conscious of the sharp vinegarish odor that rises from Cuddy's work clothes, and the image of Edna's smile clouds his vision.

"Yeah, but you'll haf ta wait till it thins out a bit," he says, not looking at the Greek.

Donny spends most of an hour joking with the workmen who come and go at the counter. By one o'clock the crowd thins out, and Albert notices that Donny keeps glancing over his shoulder at Edna who has her back to him as she moves about cleaning tables. Albert walks slowly out of the kitchen, sets the paper sack with the sandwiches next to the register and looks over at Donny.

"Ok, Mr. Grocer, yer sandwiches are all set for yah here."

The tone of his voice is flat. Against his tightly drawn cheeks, the luxuriant moustache is coal black. The Greek loses his smile, his eyes narrow a bit. He nudges Cuddy who's been sitting with his elbows on the counter gazing absently out of the lunchroom window.

"How about this guy, huh? Great service here."

Cuddy turns and looks at the two of them.

"Oh, yeah. Al's a helleva great guy. Great place here. Get anything yah want," Cuddy offers with a nod of sincere approval.

"Yessir, Al's always willin' tah go that extra mile for yah. Willin' tah share whatever's he's got." Donny's looking down at the counter, shaking his head and grinning from ear to ear.

Albert senses a movement at his elbow and turns to face Edna who's standing at the register looking at Donny.

"Whyn't yah go start cleaning up in th' back? I'll cash him out," she says without turning to her husband, who watches her faintly flushed face. Her wide eyes seem to reach out caressing the Greek.

"Well, g'wan, Al, before the grill gets cold. I'll take care of everything here." Edna's voice has a bright, girlish ring.

Donny hands Edna a couple of bucks. "Keep the change," he says softly, and then he's gone.

Albert looks around desperately. Edna is busy at the register, her back to him. Cuddy has slipped away, the lunchroom is deserted, East Main is empty of traffic, and it will be hours before Eddie returns from school. Albert walks slowly to the front window, stops and stands there gazing out, listening for the unspoken secrets of the silent street.

A Winter's Tale

That December there was no snow until New Year's Eve, and every day I'd hurry to work along bare pavement under a leaden sky. The iron picket fence on Forbes Street behind St. Mary's Church seemed a grim sentinel of the bitter mornings. Only the small neon shamrocks above Shaughnessy's Bar and the twinkling red lights in the Sears and Roebuck window relieved the grey monotony of East Main Street. When I arrived Mac's Men's Shop was always damp, the timer having just tripped on the boiler. Invariably Mac was already in the back room, sipping a steaming cup of coffee and having a pipe full of Holiday.

"Hey, Danny. How's tricks?" he'd ask.

"In one word, cold," I'd always say.

Then in silence we'd get to work, straightening up before the bells on the front door started jangling. In those days, business downtown between Christmas and New Year's was still brisk. Customers would return small items, ties, belts, cufflink sets, sport or dress shirts that were the wrong color or size. As New Year's Eve approached, a lot of the older guys who still dressed would come in for fancy formal shirts, black lisle dress socks, and cummerbunds, so we were able to put a nice finish on the year.

But that morning traffic was slow, and at noon Mac decided that his breakfast of a Sanka, black, no sugar, had played itself out. He said he'd run over to Kathy's Restaurant and get us a couple of take-out hamburger specials. After he left, I strolled down to the sock cabinet near the front door and stared out at the slowly flashing orange and blue sign of W. T. Grant's across East Main. Random snowflakes floated down sticking here and there on the grey concrete of the sidewalk. As I contemplated the lowering sky, who should shuffle up but Colley McIntyre. His shoulders were hunched against the cold as he stood chewing on his scraggly moustache and gazing vacantly into the display windows. In profile, Colley's face was birdlike. He had a turned up nose, a chin that fell rapidly away beneath thin lips, and greying hair close-cropped above the ears. On top of his head a shock of that hair stood almost straight up like a rooster's comb.

I was surprised to see Colley for rumor around downtown was that he usually spent the holidays drunk in his room over at the Y. As I watched him a memory stole over me. It was when I was just a kid, and with my father and aunt coming back from St. Patrick's Day breakfast at my cousin's house in Perth. The three of us were wedged in the front seat of the family car as we made our way along Division Street. My aunt suddenly called out,

"Oh, Michael! Look. In Grinsus' lot. Slow down!"

"What?" my father asked distractedly.

"In the parking lot, Michael. Grinsus' lot. It's Colley McIntyre. Look, fer God's sake. He's walking like he's got half a jag on! "She pushed her arm sharply against me and sat forward. I remember looking up to see a rail thin man walking stiffly as if angry or just uncertain of his ability to get to where he was going. His coat was buttoned tightly all the way to his chin which was dirtied by a sparse beard, a tuft of brown hair stood up on his head, and in his hand he clutched a small package.

"Lookit how he's staggering right in the middle of the day! He's drunk! He's drunk!" my aunt shrieked with what seemed to be delight.

"Yeah, he's drunk again, awright," my father said.

The memory faded quickly as Colley pushed against the glass of Mac's door, managed to open it, and shuffled through. Of course, I'd stepped back a couple of paces preparing myself for the aroma of stale cigarette smoke and booze that usually served as Colley's cologne of choice. But what I detected was a heavy scent of Old Spice, and when I studied his face close up I saw that the whites of his eyes weren't bloodshot, and when he spoke, he didn't stammer.

"Mac around by any chance?" he asked quietly.

"Gone for lunch, can I help you with something?"

"Hmm. Well, I guess you can. I'm in the market for a cummerbund. I think I'm probably going to need a thirty-two waist. Either black or burgundy, probably."

Off I headed to the back room to search for a thirty-two waist cummerbund. As I yanked boxes off the formal wear shelf, the doorbells jangled and I looked out to see Mac cradling a couple of brown paper bags against his chest. Colley was standing over against the shirt bins with his back to the aisle so he didn't see Mac coming toward me. Mac didn't see Colley either; he was too intent on getting our lunches into the backroom before they cooled down. The smells of french fries, ketchup, and coffee all mixed together switched my attention from the cummerbunds to food. But now that lunch was here, I decided I could be expansive, helpful. I figured the quicker we took care of this rare bird, the quicker both of us would get to eat.

"Hey Mac, Colley here needs a cummerbund, size thirty-two, black or burgundy." I called out.

“Is that so?” said Mac. “Well let’s see if we can get ol’Colley squared away here.”

Colley came up to us sheepishly.

“H-hya, Mac,” Colley stammered through a crooked grin. Mac started going through the boxes I’d placed on the register counter.

“So Colley, ya goin’ out on the town for New Years, eh?” offered Mac.

“Aw, naw. Nope. I’m helpin’ out Tommy. Ya know, Shaughnessy’s.”

“Is that right?”

“Y-yeah. Jackie and Emma are in Boston. It’s just Tommy and Ida over there, and Jackie asked me to give ‘em a hand for the holidays. Kinda take charge of the place, ya know. Jackie and Emma, they’re in Boston.” Colley repeated, eyes going wide.

“She’s got the cancer.”

“Who?” asked Mac.

“Emma, Emma Shaughnessy’s got cancer.”

“Oh.”

“Yeah, so I’m helpin’ em out tendin’ bar this afternoon and, and t-tonight.”

“Well,” said Mac, “which one do ya want? I got both black and burgundy in a thirty-two.”

“Ok, well, g-gimme the burgundy. It’ll give me some color for New Year’s Eve.”

“Right.” said Mac.

Colley gave me the money, Mac gave him the box, and I gave Colley the change. One, two, three, and, salivating like Pavlov’s dog, I headed for the back room in short order. As I tore into my lunch, I looked up to see Mac and Colley looking at one another down by the front door. Mac was filling his pipe.

"You have a nice New Years now, Colley." Mac said.

Colley's face broke into the crooked grin again.

"Sure am, Mac. I'm just gonna be doin' my job, w-watchin' all them drunks gettin' plastered."

He turned and scurried out. After Colley left, Mac turned back to me smiling with his pipe clenched between his teeth.

"Jesus," he said shaking his head.

Colley was our last customer that day. By the time I had finished off the dregs of my lukewarm coffee, the snow was so intense that the neon sign above Grant's was a dimly glowing blob of orange and blue. At four-thirty Mac decided to call it quits. I killed the radio and lights at the front, and Mac took care of the dead bolts on the back door. We wished one another well out on the sidewalk, our words muffled in the thickly falling snow. I made my way slipping along in the two or three inches of greasy slush that covered the sidewalks. The storm grew in intensity as I neared Liberty Street so that I could see hardly ten paces in front of me. An easterly wind blew the heavy snow into my face with such insistence that I tried to walk with my head down to keep the heavy flakes out of my eyes. The familiar street suddenly filled me with foreboding. I looked up fearing that out of the whiteness unseen multitudes might be bearing down on me.

The wind slackened a bit, and I saw a slim figure approaching, its right arm stretched out touching the Sears window in an attempt to steady itself on the slippery pavement. As we drew abreast of one another I saw it was Colley McIntyre and decided to give him a friendly word, something about fellow travelers caught in a storm on New

Year's Eve. In response, Colley stopped short, his right hand resting against the glass while he raised his left arm out from his side in a wobbly gesture to keep from falling backwards. As close as I was to him, I could see that the thickly falling snow had soaked through the shoulders of his thin overcoat. At first, he stared straight ahead apparently not seeing me. Then he looked in my direction. "C'mon, you son-of-bitch, you wanna fight? I'll give you a fight, if that's what you want!" he yelled. He pushed himself away from the wall with his right hand and made an ineffectual gesture with his left as if to grab me. Amazed and half afraid, I backed out of his way. Colley McIntyre turned then, and steadying himself against the building as he walked, disappeared into the storm.

Slipping through the freezing slush, I struggled toward home. The storm began to weaken rapidly, and by the time I turned the corner onto Forbes the wind had dropped. The air brightened. Before me the street lay shrouded and silent. No car tracks had disturbed the thick mantle of snow, and I couldn't tell where the sidewalk dropped down into the road. Each point of the iron pickets at the back of St. Mary's was covered in a soft blunt-ended mound of white. I looked up and saw that the breaking clouds, backlit by the setting sun, had arranged themselves like ladder rungs against the pale blue sky. To the west the storefronts along East Main Street glowed pink and gold in the early evening's tender light. I breathed deeply of the cold clear air, and felt all around me alive with the raw and unpredictable energy of life.

There Will Be Silence

A voice whispers, softly sibilant in the ear. *It is December ... December ... time for solace and surrender.* The whispering grows louder, becomes a hive of angry bees rising above his head, and Colley McIntyre wakes to see the clock dial glowing an angry orange in the middling darkness. The hour hand points to the eight, the minute stub gestures toward the numeral four. Stretching forth a bony hand, he pushes the button of the alarm. Instantly the hive is silenced. *Good enough,* he thinks, *Up early enough to make sure Cudahy ain't late this mornin'.*

Pawing back the covers, Colley stretches his legs over the mattress edge and gingerly sets his feet down onto the cold linoleum. He waits a moment to catch his breath then reaches up to grab the window shade, the damp edge of the oilcloth sticking to his fingers. He has to tug a bit to let go. The shade rises with a sharp snap, and the iron light of a winter morning washes into the room.

Colley sits hunched forward. In profile his face is birdlike, with a narrow hooked nose and a chin that falls rapidly away below thin lips. On top of his head, close cropped above the ears, a sparse shock of greying hair stands straight up like a rooster's comb. He reaches down and picks the thin overcoat that serves as his robe from off the floor, draws it about his shoulders, and stands up. The room begins to move around, and Colley abruptly sits back on the bed, waiting. The odors of whiskey, urine, and the salt of his nightsweat rise about him. Voices arise from memory to admonish and console. *Swear it off, Colley. Go on the wagon, Colley! You can do it boy! Remember, there-is-no-such-word-as-can't!*

Colley stands again, opens the door and looks toward the bathroom he shares with the other third floor boarders at the Amsterdam, New York YMCA. The lavatory door is ajar, so he takes the dusty leather shaving kit from the dresser, slips on his unlaced brogans, and swaying a bit, makes his way down the deserted hall.

Long and narrow the bathroom lies before him. A hard, unforgiving light shines through the window of frosted glass above the grey zinc tub. The mirror over the sink catches his reflection, and a former schoolteacher and current fulltime drunk stares back at Colley. *Well,* he thinks, *there'll be no wiping of the suds about the cheeks this morning for the month's growth of beard is patchy enough as it is. Just a quick touch along the neck will do, then over to the Pink and Rock for breakfast.*

Colley hurries through the front door of the Y into the empty street. The sky is cloudless, and the bright winter sun just clearing the rooftops of Fownes Glove Company along the north side of East Main Street makes his eyes water. He looks down and hurries forward, feeling every crack and groove of the icy pavement through his thin shoe soles. *December thirty-first already and still no snow. Who coulda imagined! Well, if it kin get to th' end of the year without snowing, other amazing things are no doubt gonna happen, too.* Colley, chin up, gives a nod of approbation to the glowing sun.

At the intersection of Church and East Main he's brought up short by a yellow New York Central Railroad truck starting to move through the green light. Suddenly the truck stops, and Colley, blinking away cold tears, looks up to see two gandy dancers peering down at him. Colley's gaze passes quickly over Bernie Andrulis in the passenger seat, and fixes on the scowling driver, big Eddie Geiger, working furiously at the shift lever. Bernie wheels down the window.

"G'wan Colley," he barks, waving a gloved hand.

Colley manages a quick smile and wave at Eddie. Then he looks straight ahead, gulps down a mouthful of frigid air and runs past the truck. At his back he hears Eddie gunning the engine, the gears grinding as the truck moves off west toward the train station.

The Pink and Rock is quiet. Tom Cudahy, the barman and nephew of Jack and Emma Ryan, the owners, is already in. Cudahy is bending over the bar sink, and Colley's gaze goes directly to the mural painted across the wall above Tom's head. Seascape of sky and water boiling around a naked nubile virgin chained to rocks in the foreground. Pink breasts and thighs unscathed above the crashing waves and jagged stone. "Legend of Theseus" reads the large brass colored plate below the center of the work. *Paint me Aeolus above and nice pink teats and ass below,* thinks Colley, smiling.

Tom Cudahy looks up from behind the bar.

"How'se boy?" barks Colley.

"Ohhhhhhh-Kay." says Tom, looking down, busying himself at the sink.

"Dja order the meat?"

"Yeah."

How about Eber's order?"

"Yeah. Be here Thursday. "Six cases of mixed and six kegs. Three on tap and three in reserve. Same again the following week."

"Bread order?"

Tom looks up at Colley. Cudahy is a slightly built, small featured man with neatly trimmed black hair, elephant-like ears which stick out horizontally, and a thin moustache that almost succeeds in spreading itself across his upper lip. Colley looks at the younger man's face, as smooth and wrinkleless as a young boy's. Tom has an odd habit of pulling his mouth down at the corners when he is about to speak, as though he is about to utter a curse or give some indispensable bit of advice. His dark eyes stare at Colley and the corners of his mouth begin their downward dance.

"I took care of everything," he says quietly.

"Sure ya did. I, I know ya did, Tommy. I was jest checkin' cause Jackie w-wanted me to," Colley offers. Tommy drops his eyes and goes back to his machinations at the sink.

Colley sits down on a stool at the end of the bar, his shoulders sagging.

After a while Tom calls out, "Hey, ya want just a little of the usual?"

"Hell, no. Gimme a couple a them hardboiled eggs and a big mug a joe, black. I'm goin' on the wagon."

"Again, huh?"

Colley brightens.

"Yep. Gotta look after you, boy, like I promised Jackie and Emma. Friends got to look out fer one another in tough times. Especially now, with Emma's cancer n' all. That woman's Jackie's pillar of strength. Behind every man there's a woman. Somewhere--mother, wife, girl friend, I don't care.

Men are the weaker sex. If Emma don't pull through, what th' hell's gonna happen to this place?"

"Yah don't say?" Cudahy puts a plate of two colored pickled eggs in front of Colley. Next to it he deftly slides a brimful mug of black coffee. He regards Colley with a guarded stare.

"It's more than just this place. Look what they did for you after all yer screwups."

"Yeah, don't I know it. Sometimes I think my life's writ large in missed opportunities," sniffs Colley apologetically.

"Sure," says Tommy, growing expansive. "Lookit what they did for you years ago specially with that Kate Ambrose mess."

"Yeah," says Colley. "Course that's all old business. Unfinished business, of course, but old business, back in the past, my boy. Over and done with long ago."

"Yeah, well, ya know what they say, huh, Colley?" Tommy smirks. "Unfinished business is the only business. Anyway, Emma and Jackie'll be back from Boston end of January. She'll be ok. Don't be such a worrier. You think too much," the corners of Tommy's mouth are still down, his dark eyes fixed on Colley.

The door to the bar swings inward with a faint hiss. At this hour Colley knows it's Ida, the hostess, waitress, and gatekeeper of the Pink and Rock. *If she likes you, you're in. If not, well, you're permanently east of Eden.* He swivels on the bar stool and faces the short, amply endowed blonde. Ida's green eyes come to rest on Colley. Her mouth is set in a subtle grin of contentment, neither cynical nor self-serving. It says to Colley that Ida Payzak is ok with the world.

"Hi-ya guys."

"Ida," says Tommy.

"Good morning, Miss Payzak."

Ida pads up to Colley on soft-soled snow boots. In her hands she clutches an oversize black purse which contains, Colley guesses, her work shoes and whatever else it is that women carry in those things.

"My, ain't we formal this mornin', perfessor."

She squints a bit as she smiles up at him.

"How're ya feelin'' this morning, Colley? You don't look so good but I see ya got yer breakfast there. Are ya ok?"

"I'm fine. Matter of fact, I'm goin' on the wagon. Turnin' over a new leaf for the new year. I just tole Tommy. Ya think I can do it, Ida?"

"I sure hope so Colley. It'd be wonderful if you could. Yer educated. You can do anything you put yer mind to, I'm sure. I really mean that Colley."

Ida turns to Tommy.

"Tommy, look what I got!"

From her purse she draws a brown cardboard box, setting it on the bar.

"I got these practically fer free from Lurie's. They were the last two. I took the liberty of puttin' 'em on the store account cause they were so cheap."

She pulls the wrapping paper from two grapefruit-size ornamental glass balls. One says "Happy" and the other "New Year" in frosted white script on a deep red background. The corners of Tommy's mouth drop down a bit.

"Where we gonna put 'em, Ida?"

"On either side of the painting." She gestures up at Ariadne in chains. Tommy looks from Ida to Ariadne and back to Ida. The corners of his mouth sag even lower.

"Ok, if that's what you want, do it," he says turning back to the sink.

Colley studies the ornaments for a moment, then looks at his plate of eggs. One is green, and the other a dark red much like the color of the glass balls that Ida is now attempting to attach with neatly cut pieces of masking tape to either side of the Legend of Theseus. Colley slices through the rubbery white flesh and down into the dry yellow-green yolk. The eggs break into crumbling, jagged-edged pieces. He looks at them and decides he's more thirsty than he is hungry.

"Hey, Colley, waddya think? " Ida has taped the wire hooks on top of the Christmas balls to the frame on either side of the painting. She's watching him from behind the bar.

"Huh?"

"Hey, c'mon. Aintcha gonna eat those eggs?"

"S-Sure, I'm gonna eat my eggs, an' them ornaments look just fine."

Tommy and Ida disappear into the kitchen. Colley picks up the plate and coffee cup and shuffles over to his usual table by the window. The sky has clouded over and looking through the glass he can see the front of Luries Department Store on the opposite side of East Main. The display windows glow warmly in red and white holiday lights, but the rows of windows on the upper floors are cold black holes in the grey brick wall. Downtown is deserted and the silence of the street seems to creep slowly into the Pink and Rock as Colley's gaze turns to the rows of bottles arranged below The Legend of Theseus.

The door hisses and he looks up to see a young couple standing at the far end of the row of tables. They're both bare-headed and dressed in dark pea coats above faded jeans. Colley knows they're not local. The guy, who's tall with shoulder-length blonde hair, notices Colley and begins to move forward, the girl following close behind. They stop in front of him, and the guy bends forward, his hands splayed out on the tabletop. Colley sees that the nails of his left hand are closely trimmed, but the ones on the right are long and carefully manicured. *Musician. Hippies just passing through*, he thinks.

"Can ya tell me how I'd get to th' Armory from here?"

The big fellow's voice is surprisingly high, almost a falsetto. Colley looks up at the face, pimply, flushed a bright red by the damp cold.

"Sure can, young fellow. Yah just go west on East Main here til yah get to th' corner of Market and take a left over the river bridge. The Armory's right in front of yah, just up th' hill after yah get off the bridge."

The young man straightens up and turns to the girl. The mass of his broad shoulders shifts under the close fitting wool of his coat, and just before he speaks Colley notices the muscles working under the skin of his square jaw.

"See, I tolja I was right. Th' Armory is on the other side of the river."

The voice is petulant. Almost a whine. Colley turns his attention to the girl. She's short, coming just above the big guy's elbow. Her long hair is jet black, the face sharp featured, with a nose slightly hooked. In profile her lips are full and the cold has given the smooth skin of her cheek a flush.

"Yeah. I forgot. You're always right," she says in a voice deeper than the guy's and richly sensual. She turns her dark eyes briefly on Colley and turns again focusing her gaze out the window, a slight smile playing about her lips. The tone of that low voice opens a wound in Colley's memory. He looks down and sees that she has placed her ungloved hand on the back of the chair in front of him. Her white fingers, long and with a delicate taper ending in finely sculpted nails seem to glow in the light. In the eye of memory Colley sees Kate Ambrose's face with the same dark eyes and hair. He sees the same exquisite hand. He hears the same voice of infinite promise. Colley draws back, and nods, looking at the boy.

"Yeah, yeah, yer right. The Armory's always been on the Southside. Used ta be a real armory way back, around th' time of the Civil War. Then it became a dance hall. Heh, yeah, fancy place when I was yer age. Used tah go there all th' time fer big dances. Got decent food, c-can't say nuthin' bad about it."

The girl turns and begins slowly walking toward the door. The boy follows her. Colley sits, silent, staring through the window at the young couple as they climb into a small car parked at the curb. He hears the engine start and watches as the car moves away.

Ida emerges from the kitchen.

"Who was that?"

"Just some kids askin' directions."

"Yuh gonna come back and help us out? "

He stares at her.

"Colley…?"

"Ah, nah. I'm just gonna sit here I think an' greet whoever starts showin' up. Gotta put a friendly face on for th' clientele this time a year, yah know."

He can see those wide green eyes on him and he tries a wink in her direction.

"Well, ok," Ida says staring at him. "Yah said things were changin', an' I believe yah. We're countin' on yah, Colley, an' I know that if we all pull together we kin make Emma an' Jackie proud."

Ida stares at him searching his face as he holds her gaze, forcing himself not to turn away. Then she slips into the kitchen, and Colley hears the rattle of pans back there. *Must be gettin' the sausage an' macaroni ready. Course, why would anybody'd be interested in eatin' on New Year's Eve? Now that's a time for a liquid celebration. What th' hell! Once a year!* Colley looks at the tiers of bottles lined up across the back bar. They glow warmly in red and yellow, green and quicksilver, bejeweled with the promise of untold possibilities. New Year! New Start! Colley raises his head and feels himself worthy of accepting any challenge.

Time passes and the noises from the kitchen gradually subside. Colley looks anxiously at the bits of egg on his plate, the pale traces of red and green smudged across the white china. They whisper in the language of broken things, painting pictures in long-lost summer colors: green leaves and skies a muted crimson at twilight. He can smell the musky fragrance of perfumed hair, feel the faint breeze that comes with sunset and the delicate pressure of a gentle hand along his forearm. Dark eyes full of promise turn upon him. But then he hears a bitter voice declaiming, *Drunks and barflies always find each other.*

"Not for anything did I want that to happen," Colley whispers to the bottles above the bar, and suddenly the door behind him hisses. He jumps at the sound and turns to see big Eddie Geiger standing alone just inside the entrance.

"Hey, Eddie. How th' hell are yah? Bernie ain't with yah, hunh?"

"Nah. Yah know Kate won't let 'im drink. Not even at New Year's fer Chris' sake."

Eddie pushes past him and makes for the bar.

"Cold as a you know what out there this mornin'. Ah think maybe these old bones are in need of a little Southern Comfort," Eddie calls over his shoulder.

"Shit, don't I know that. What can I getcha?"

Colley scurries from his table, rounds the end of the bar, and faces Eddie, who's a head taller sitting on a stool than Colley is standing. Eddie looks at the row of bottles along the wall, his eyes narrow slits of concentration in his puffy, dough-colored face.

"Gimme a double of th' Jameson's."

"Ah, yer goin' with th' Irish, uh. Yeah, yah don't want none a that sugar water. That's a liquor fer sissies anyway. It's ok fer th' South where it's warm, but up here yah … "

"And a schooner of whatever's cheap that ya got on tap."

"Oh, oh yeah sure, comin' right up. Time t' celebrate."

Colley reaches for the Jameson's bottle and two double shot glasses on the back bar. He sets one glass before Eddie and fills it to the brim, then turns, grabs a beer glass and moves over to the first tap. He places the full schooner next to the shot in front of Eddie, reaches down under the counter and fills the second shot half way from the whiskey bottle.

"Yer joinin' me?"

"Yeah, what th' hell," Colley nods in the direction of the kitchen door, "they ain't payin' me tuh help 'im today. I'm just gonna have short one."

Eddie breaks into a grin and shakes his head appreciatively.

"Same old Colley. Yah ain't never gonna change." He slaps a twenty on the bar with a pawlike hand.

"Let's see how far 'at's gonna take me this afternoon."

Eddie downs the shot and reaches for his beer.

The door to the kitchen swings out and Ida emerges smiling, carrying a covered tray. Her eyes take in Eddie and the smile fades. Ida sets the tray down on the far end of the counter, and nodding, looks at big Eddie, her face placid.

"Eddie Geiger," she says. It's a simple statement of fact.

"Hey Ida. Hap…happy New Year," Eddie manages to sputter out as he carefully lowers the empty beer glass, avoiding her frank stare. Ida turns and goes back through the kitchen door. Colley reaches down below the counter and pours himself a double. Eddie swings about on his stool pushing the empty glasses toward Colley.

"My money's still on the bar," he says.

Time passes. Through the window Colley notices that a windless snow has begun to fall, the large flakes descending so rapidly that a heavy grey curtain seems hung beyond the glass. The Jameson's works its familiar magic as the bar begins to fill with customers. When the office at Fownes Glove Company lets out, a lot of young clerks show up intent on starting the party early and, maybe, finding someone to stay with until the end. Colley looks on as they jostle one another at the bar, their faces bright with the cold and their looks hungry in anticipation. Then the office girls arrive and sit at the tables in clusters of two or three chatting excitedly. They glance at the young men repeatedly. Colley watches Ida moving among the tables, smiling in a motherly way at the young excited faces about her. Eddie Geiger's eyes follow Ida, but when she looks at the bar, her glance passes over him as if he isn't there. Colley bends, takes another shot of whiskey and looks up expecting the warm noise to rise and cover him in yet another layer of comfort. But the Pink and Rock is too quiet, the bar lights too bright. The Jameson's has stopped working, and Colley sees the needy, stray-dog looks in the young clerk's eyes. He watches the girls' reactions. Some return the looks with a soft, doe-eyed expression of acceptance, but many offer only the cool gaze of appraisal. It is a waiting game and Colley knows that many will wait too long. He's suddenly angry at the Jameson's, angry at Tommy and Ida, angry at the mill town dive that is The Pink and Rock, and angry most of all at Eddie Geiger's doughy face floating now before him, the eyes tearful slits above a mouth working stupidly in drunken grief.

"Why she hate me? Why she hate me?"

"Faint heart ne'er won fair maid. Yah didn't ask her when you should have," he spits the words in Eddie's face.

The big man takes offense. His jaws clench and eyes widen in a knowing stare. He leans in close.

"Oh yeah? Listen up, pants pisser. Least I didn't lose what I already had. Well, Bernie got her and left yah out in the cold. Hah!"

Eddie draws himself up above the bar, his lips forming a crooked grin of triumph.

Colley looks around. The Pink and Rock has disappeared. It is another December evening as Kate turns her face to his, her white hand grasping his arm. *Is it so much to ask that you not come to my door drunk and get drunker at the Armory and, in front of me and all my friends, piss your pants? Go, be with the drunks and barflies!*

"Not for anything, not for anything did I want that to happen!" Colley shouts. The customers at the bar raise their chins, cast glances of cool wariness in his direction. Couples at the closest tables stop talking and turn slowly toward him. Eddie Geiger's face closes in, his eyes wide with concern.

"Huh? What th' hell yah yellin' about, yah crazy drunk? C'mon, git yerself together. Have another shot. No hard feelin's, right? It's th' holiday."

Colley looks past Eddie. He sees Tom Cudahy approaching from the far end of the bar, his dark eyes unblinking and the corners of his mouth down.

"Hey Colley, how many bottles of the Jamesons we got left there, buddy?"

"I ain't drunk," says Colley.

Now Cudahy comes in so close that Colley can see every hair in the thin moustache.

"You ain't been drinkin' tea all afternoon. How about waitin" on some of the other customers. We got a good crowd here, I don't want no problems. I thought yah were gonna help us out here today?"

Ida comes over and sets a tray of empty glasses on the bar.

"Refills," she says to Tommy and then quickly settles her green eyes on Colley.

"Look, Tommy, I-I just can't do this right now," says Colley.

He wants to talk about the looks he's seen in the faces of the clerks and office girls, about the gaze Eddie keeps fixed on Ida, and the way Ida's eyes see everything in the Pink and Rock except Eddie Geiger. But the silence of promises unfulfilled that the Jameson's can't cut through has him staring dumbly at Tommy's beardless chin.

"Jeezuss Christ," Cudahy rasps out.

Ida puts her hand on Tommy's arm.

"It's ok, Tommy."

She faces Colley and takes hold of both his hands.

"Ya don't want to be here any more, do yah, Colley? It's ok if yah don't. Things always have a way of ending themselves. There's nothing else to say, right perfessor?"

Ida gives him a forgiving smile.

Colley holds her gaze for a long moment, then lets go of Ida's hands and wanting to keep the warmth of her consolation close about him quickly buttons up his overcoat. He turns, stumbles from behind the bar and moves toward the door. The revelers give him a wide berth.

Outside Colley McIntyre slips along the sidewalk. The snow is so heavy that it sticks to his eyelashes and beard, making it hard for him to see and breathe. He gives up trying to reach the Y, and stopping, places his hands against the dun colored brick of Fownes' mill wall. He closes his eyes and stands very still listening to the whisper of the thickly falling snow.

Daniel Cochran, A Tale Of Youth

The seven o'clock Mass was sparsely attended and the cool stillness made the atmosphere inside St. Mary's church luminous. In the dark recesses of the vaulted ceiling the narrow chandeliers glowed a bright yellow-orange. Shafts of light from the newly-risen sun slanted through the glass panels of the side door sharply etching the red and black veins of the marble floor. When Monsignor Connell and his servers emerged from the sacristy door, the light shimmered on their white vestments like a summer sun reflected off the surface of calm water. Daniel Cochran felt sure this was a special time, a time when he could see his world with absolute clarity.

The first bars of *Christ The Lord Is Risen Today* sounded from the back of the church, and Daniel turned to catch a glimpse of old Mrs. Coppard, the organist, squatting before the keyboard. The bulge on her humpback jutted up so high it hid from view all but a sliver of her grey-blue hair. Daniel stood and squared his shoulders feeling their bulk press snugly against the material of his coat.

He looked good this Easter Sunday. Even his father had as much as said so when Daniel had taken the dark brown fedora out of the hatbox that had *Dobbs Fifth Avenue* lettered so neatly in yellow cursive round the black circumference of the lid. Clearing his throat while he cast a hurried glance at

Daniel, the elder Cochran had stutteringly offered, "Th-tha-that'll look nice with the tan topcoat."

Well, of course it did. Daniel had come to realize of late how timidly his father offered his opinions. It was the stuttering that made it that way. Thankfully he didn't have that problem and was always able to speak his thoughts right out without the slightest hesitation. Daniel took a deep breath and felt his chest expand. Glancing to the side, he noted that at fifteen he could already look right over the old man's receding hairline. The hymn shuddered to a close as old Coppard held the last chord a few seconds longer than usual while Monsignor Connell, leaning heavily on his cane, ascended the steps of the altar. The priest's sloping shoulders and mass of white hair made him seem twice as broad as the two young servers at his side. Connell turned to face the congregation revealing the milky white cast that completely covered his left eye. Daniel remembered being terrified of it. But that was when he was much younger.

When it came time for the sermon, Monsignor Connell pulled himself up the pulpit's corkscrew stairs. His large hands grasped the rail as he leaned forward into the light. The sunlight had lost its gentle gold. It was acetylene now, blazing across the grey hair, and setting cold fire to the cast in the eye. Connell raised his prominent chin. In the light his head appeared to Daniel the incarnation of some marble bust from antiquity come to voice eternal truths. Spreading his arms in Christlike supplication, the priest brought his hands together in a sweeping arc that encompassed the small congregation, seeming to draw them in against his expansive chest.

"In the name of the Father and of the Son and of the Holy Spirit, Amen," Connell's deep voice filled the church.

He broke into a wide smile, the white light glinting on his large, squarely cut teeth.

"My dear brothers and sisters in Christ, may the joy of this Easter flood into our hearts as this glorious light of morning floods into our church. May it show us the way through the labyrinth of doubt and sorrow where the unkind words or looks or actions of others, and even our own dark thoughts often cloud our vision of a blessed, purposeful life."

The play of light, the imposing figure and rhythmic voice of Connell lulled Daniel into the grandeur of vaguely imagined possibilities. His reverie soon turned to Marilyn, wife of the owner of Sal's East Main Newsroom and Coffee Shop. She was a tall athletic girl much younger than her husband. Daniel figured she was just a few years older than he was, and he liked watching her. He liked the deliberate, graceful way she moved about behind the counter, like a leopard passing, sleek and sure, before its lair. Comments he'd once heard about her somewhere in the street crossed his mind stirring the ache of desire in his heart.

"Yeah, that's Roginski's daughter. Ol' Sal, he's got his hands full, all right. Got himself a young wife to take care of. Once a night ain't enough there, that's fer sure."

Daniel let his memory play over an encounter he'd had with Marilyn one warm Sunday morning just a month before. He remembered striding through the open door of Sal's and approaching the counter with a couple of quarters for the paper. He had watched Marilyn turning to him as if in slow motion. The whites of her eyes seemed to sparkle through the blue haze. Daniel saw the dark grain of her long coffee and cream colored hair, parted in the middle and combed back behind finely sculpted ears. As she leaned toward him to take the money, the hair cascaded forward, gently caressing her softly molded cheek. Smiling, she had looked up at Daniel, who saw the moist highlights on her pale pink lips and the glint of light on her teeth. Diamonds in the dusty, smoke-filled air. Marilyn's eyes had held his for a long moment, their expression neither wary nor apathetic as were the glances of girls his own age. Her look was open and direct, and just for him.

"Good morning," she had said softly, and then looked down.

"Good morning," Daniel had said, surprised at the loudness of his own voice. Squaring his shoulders and holding his head high, he had passed through the open door of the newsroom.

His reverie ceased with the end of the Mass, and Daniel followed his father into the sun-filled street announcing, "I'm goin' to Sal's fer the paper."

"Oh, oh-oh-kay. Well, see you home then." His father turned away, and stoop-shouldered, started up the walk between church and rectory, toward a covered wooden stairwell that everyone in the neighborhood called the subway leading to Forbes Avenue. Above the diminishing figure of his father, Daniel could see the rooflines of the houses on Forbes. Higher still were successive rows of light green tree tops along Grove and High Streets, their newly budded branches sharply etched against the clear Spring sky. He turned and started walking along East Main toward Sal's.

Daniel pulled a paper from the full rack outside. Behind the closed door the interior of the newsroom was a dark mystery. Entering, he saw that the stools along the lunch counter were unoccupied, and there appeared to be no one around as far back as he could see. But as he walked forward, he became aware of a movement on the floor near the far end of the counter. In an instant the movement resolved itself into the figure of a rummy-looking man Daniel had never seen before. He was lying on his back. His legs were bent at the knees, and his pants had ridden high to reveal a pair of narrow blue-splotched shins. His shoes, the edges of their soles worn razor-thin, looked as though they had been hewn out of rotten wood. The man clutched his arms about his chest as he rocked far over from side to side. His head moved in rhythm with the rocking of his body, and each time one of his cheeks touched the floor, he spit. A thin vomit glistened about his mouth and sparsely bearded chin as he stuck his tongue far out between his lips.

Stiff-legged, Daniel walked past the man, and suddenly Marilyn emerged from the telephone booth halfway back in the shop. She held the receiver in her left hand, its cord stretched tight. She seemed riveted to where she stood, unwilling to approach any nearer to him yet unable to go back into the booth. The light and dark strands of her brown hair were matted on the sweat of her brow. Marilyn stared at him with eyes wide in angry fear.

"Fer God's sake," she yelled, "get somebody. Jesus Christ, get somebody! Help me here! Can't you help me here?"

Daniel stood looking at Marilyn. Slowly he stretched forth his hand, and let the quarters fall to the floor at her feet. Then he turned and ran past the writhing sufferer and out of the shop, slamming the door behind him. He found himself back in front of St. Mary's before he stopped, Marilyn's cry, "Can't you help me here?" echoing in his ears.

Sweating, Daniel took his hat off and looked around, unsure of where he was going. The harsh glare of the sun nearly blinded him. The line of tree tops above Grove and

High Streets appeared a dull grey, their edges indistinct, and the entrance to the subway was now a dark hole of uncertain possibilities. Dazed, he made his way home.

In the bright light of late morning, Daniel sat at the small kitchen table, wedging his chair against the side of the humming refrigerator. He leaned back, seeking comfort in the incessant gentle vibration along his back. The room was silent, save for the gentle whoosh of the gas oven and the occasional crackle of ham roasting for Easter dinner. Daniel's eyelids drooped. He squinted, peering through the glass panes of the kitchen door at the backyard's old stonewall. In the sunlight the sharp lines of white mortar coursing between the lopsided slabs of grey fieldstone made the surface of the wall look like a trackless maze drawn on the smudged surface of wrinkled paper. An agony of self-doubt consumed him. Suddenly he felt the forceful step of his mother entering the room.

"Whatsa matter, Danny, yuh been so quiet all morning. Yuh ain't even looked at th' paper. Somethin' happen at Sal's?"

Her voice was an uncharacteristic mixture of querulousness and concern.

"Nah," he said, then hesitated, certain that revealing what had happened at the newsroom would bring only the usual list of recriminations, and advice. Without turning to her he replied,

"Nuthin' happened. Why are yuh asking me that?"

No reply came and Daniel heard the shuffle of his father's footsteps. His mother began to move busily from stove to sink.

"So, how'd old Connell do at the seven-o'clock? It's a miracle he kin get around anymore, if yuh ask my opinion," his mother declared.

"W-well, he did ok. Course, he's got th' others tuh take the later Masses, an' bein' Monsignor an' all, he can pretty much call the shots about when he wants tuh say Mass," his father conceded.

"Yeah, an don't ferget he's got his own housekeeper over there at the Rectory," his mother said.

Daniel turned to watch them. His father's chin was raised, eyes wide and high forehead wrinkled. Daniel detected a plaintive note of supplication in his voice.

"W-well, it's still gotta be tough on 'im, even with old Miss Walsh. W-went to school with both of 'im jist before he left fer th' seminary. Boy, he sure wasn't happy about that. But what could he do? Blind in one eye and all. O-of course, it is jus' the two of 'im now, and w-whose it hurt after all this time, anyway?"

"Oh, when they were young we called her somethin' else! Him too! But it's th' housekeeper, now," his mother snapped back.

"Well, he was never a happy man. Don't s'pose either one of 'em has ever been happy," his father said quietly.

After dinner Daniel sat alone in the small living room. His father had disappeared and the faint clattering of his mother in the kitchen seemed to reinforce the heavy silence. The morning's disaster at Sal's crept insistently into his thoughts. It was the cowardice of a boy that had made him run from Marilyn. He feared that he'd never again be able to enter Sal's and face the questioning, pitying look she was sure to fix upon him. Daniel grew restless and decided he had to see what disaster his lack of action at Sal's had caused. He had to get a look at the outside of the newsroom. He could get a quick view of the entrance to Sal's from in front of Saint Mary's Rectory. See if anybody was around the place. If he lost his nerve, he could just come back home and wait for time to pass. Maybe someday, when he was a man, he'd have the guts to go in and explain it all to Marilyn.

Outside the sky had clouded over and the wind had begun to rise. As he walked cautiously along Main Street, Daniel saw two darkly clad figures linked arm in arm walking toward him from in front of the high concrete wall topped by iron pickets which enclosed the Rectory grounds. The figures moved cautiously, like two flightless birds just escaped from a cage. Daniel could see the purple tassel atop the black cap of the shorter figure, and he knew the couple must be Monsignor Connell and the housekeeper, Miss Walsh. His heart quickened at the certainty that their paths would cross. Daniel suddenly realized he had encountered Connell only from afar. St. Mary's had many parishioners and neither he nor his parents were among the important members of the congregation. How should he greet them? Walking quickly by the pair with eyes averted was something a child would do, like running away from another's cry for help. But what could he say? He decided to wait until the pair came up to him, for Connell would know what to say once he got close enough, and Daniel could get a good look at Miss Walsh. The words of his mother, "oh, we called her somethin' else then, him too" sounded again in his ears. What were they to one another? He'd never heard the housekeeper spoken of in the neighborhood.

The priest and Miss Walsh drew near. Monsignor Connell was a full head shorter than Daniel and the black cassock he wore was buttoned tightly about his chest. His mass of grey hair was unkempt and curiously dry looking in the fretful, humid air. Tottering a bit from side to side, the priest moved forward awkwardly, all his attention focused on the pavement in front of him.

Miss Walsh was as tall as Daniel, with a slim, boyish figure. She wore a short- sleeved blouse of dark red and a long black skirt that came nearly to her ankles. Her lean arms were large-veined and sinewy with age. Yet they seemed to glow against the dark colored clothing. Connell clung to her, his large, soft-looking hand nearly encircling her raised forearm.

Miss Walsh's very black hair was straight and cut short. Its deep color made a striking contrast to the shiny, nearly transparent skin of her face. When they drew abreast of one another, she stopped. Her grey eyes fixed on Daniel with a steady open look that suggested acceptance instead of challenge.

"Now, what is your name, young man?"

As she spoke wrinkles blossomed in the skin around her thin-lipped mouth.

"Cochran, Daniel Cochran," said Daniel, thinking that his voice sounded apologetic.

"And are you a member of Saint Mary's?" Miss Walsh nodded, inviting his reply.

"Oh, yes," said Daniel.

"See," Miss Walsh addressed her companion, nodding in Daniel's direction, "what did I tell you? Such a fine-looking young man! I knew he belonged to the parish the moment I saw him coming toward us."

"Yes, you're right," agreed the priest, letting go of Miss Walsh's arm and looking up. Daniel could see that the cast froze Connell's blind eye in place, but his good eye moved about, taking in all around him. His gaze swept briefly over Daniel, then settled upon Miss Walsh's face.

"Your eyesight is much better than mine ever was," he said with a wan smile revealing long, loose-seeming teeth. He turned back to Daniel.

"So," he began, then paused, the good eye regarding Daniel with a vacant stare, "Cochran … Cochran. Does your family live close by?" Connell's voice sounded thin and reedy.

"Yes," said Daniel, "up on Forbes Street."

"Well," said the priest, "living so close to the church, I'm sure you're a fine member of our parish. And a good boy."

"Yes, Father," offered Daniel, looking down. In the silence that followed, he raised his eyes to see Connell, tight-lipped, nodding at him, apparently satisfied by the aptness of his own judgment.

"Well, that's it, isn't it? You are a good boy." The Monsignor gave a final, decisive nod at Daniel, his face sealing itself off as if it were the entrance to an ancient tomb.

"Of course he's a good boy. Anyone can see that," said Miss Walsh, smiling brightly at Daniel. He noticed the deep lines at the corners of her eyes and the creases descending from the corners of her mouth to end in the hint of jowls on either side of her narrow chin. Yet her pale face shone as her eyes sought him out. For a long moment, she held Daniel's gaze without reservation or embarrassment, as though she was trying to make of him a newly found friend.

"Shouldn't we be getting back? This young man ought to be getting on home in case the rain begins," ventured the priest.

Miss Walsh bent forward, turning Connell back across the parking lot. After a few steps, she looked over her shoulder.

"Perhaps another day we'll see you when we're out walking. Or you can come to the rectory. Don't let the iron bars scare you away. We're always open to a visit from parishioners. It helps Father stay in touch with the people."

Daniel watched the priest and his housekeeper cross East Main Street. They made their way through the opening in the concrete wall and up the front steps of the Rectory. Connell ducked in at the door, but Miss Walsh hesitated, her tall figure standing as though on guard before a refuge. She raised her open hand in a bright blossom of a wave. Emboldened, Daniel held his hand high, palm outstretched as well, returning her gesture. Then she too disappeared.

Daniel turned to look at the front of Sal's. All was quiet there, the sidewalk deserted, the news rack still full of papers fluttering in the rising breeze. Above him a shining patch of blue sky appeared, tunneling through the maze of clouds. Brightness seemed to fall from the air. It occurred to Daniel that the earlier events at Sal's just might have consequences that only a boy would worry about. He turned around, and with deliberate steps, made for the entrance of the subway.

Ash Wednesday, A Boy's Memory

In memory he always has about him the powerful yet elegant air of the boxer. Stepping briskly through the sacristy door, Father Magielda moves toward the marble study of the Sacred Heart of Jesus. The statue itself appears to acknowledge the special energy of the priest. The large expressive eyes, full-lipped mouth, and the outstretched palms thrust forward to display the stigmata seem to give a visual representation of the Biblical injunction, "Behold, the man!" at Magielda's approach. As he passes in front of the figure, the priest turns slightly toward the congregation, his shoulders obscuring for a moment the inscription, "Mercy for My Lambs," cut in dull bronze Black Letter across the statue's massive pedestal. With shoulders squared, chin thrust forward, and hands clasped high across his breast, Magielda turns and quickly approaches the middle of the sanctuary. In profile his face slopes gently forward from the brow. The nose is slightly hooked and below its bulbous tip his mouth curves downward a bit to meet the jowl line of his cheek. As he reaches the center of the sanctuary, he pivots to the right, bringing his left foot in a graceful arc onto the first step leading to the high altar.

The broad movement of his square shoulders and hips beneath surplice and cassock suggests the strength of Magielda's body. Ascending the altar's steps, he seems to dodge and feint from side to side. The skirt of the cassock dances about his heels. Magielda reaches the top step, rises to his full height, and spreads his arms outward across the edge of the altar shelf. With head bent to the left and hands set firmly on the white altar cloth, he genuflects, rises again and opens the door of the tabernacle. The reflected light of the tall altar candles shines upon the bald spot above his neatly tonsured greying hair like the tongues of fire I have seen over the Apostle's heads in a painting of the Epiphany.

When Father Magielda genuflects again, I can see the ornate chalice, its surface shimmering in the light like a golden flame. He rises, stands still, head thrown back a bit, as if he were in communion with some unseen presence hovering above. Then his tall form hunches slightly forward over the chalice. The tongue of fiery light gleams on his balding head. I stare at it for a moment, and close my eyes savoring the grey-green after-image.

At once I am aware of the low murmur of the people surrounding me. Someone sneezes, a child's muted cry rises from the back of St. Mary's Church, and the sibilance of an old woman's lips as she says her rosary kneeling in the pew in front of me reach my ears. Wrapped in a worn black coat and with her head covered by a greasy grey scarf, the old woman rocks gently to and fro, in rhythm with the cadence of her prayer.

To my left my mother moves furtively. All winter she has worn a thin coat of brown cotton suede, and now in her catlike self-possession she sits with her hands crossed and drawn up into the sleeves. The abstracted quality of her eyes as they glance about the scene suggests a weary indifference to the ritual of Ash Wednesday.

Father Magielda stands tall and still as the servers busy themselves opening the low railing. He steps through the open gate as the congregation rises to meet him.

The grey-scarved woman in front of me stands with an alacrity incongruous for her age, darts out of the pew and pushes into the crowd ahead of her. The sound of many other hurried footsteps strike forcefully on the wooden floor like the rumble of distant thunder. I can see Father Magielda jostled from side to side as the crowd surges forward. A fetid odor sweeps back toward me from the mass of eager parishioners swarming about the priest.

Dark red patches mottle Father Magielda's face. The corners of his mouth bend lower and the wrinkles on either side of his chin become dark creases. His eyes grow wide. Raising himself up and away from the people pressing upon him he thunders,

"You people! Go back to your seats! I will not have this stampeding like cattle! You are in the House of God."

All of Father's energy is concentrated in the depths of his voice, terrible now with rage.

"I will not conduct this service for a mob of brutish louts!"

Quickly and furtively the parishioners spread away from the priest. The old woman in the dirty scarf darts into the pew immediately in front of Magielda. One elderly man, his white hair streaked with yellow and grey, stands at the entrance to a pew, staring in Magielda's direction. His small eyes set deeply into a florid face reflect a mixture of shock and uncertainty. Then he too slips into a seat. The altar boys stand stiffly at Father's side, their eyes cast down and their red, hot faces betraying a mixture of embarrassment and fear.

My cheeks burn as though they had been slapped. Father Magielda now seems far down the aisle, yet his presence rises gigantically before the altar. As I look around, each face in the congregation seems shiny-eyed and ablaze in the violent light of the priest's anger. For a moment I feel burdened by a terrible need to shape this event in my mind. But in an instant I feel my attention slip from all I have seen and I can only think of the faint salty odor of my own unwashed hair and the musty smell of my coat. A bead of sweat trickles slowly from the back of my neck downward between my shoulder blades.

The church is silent. Father turns, and with long strides moves back behind the altar rail. The servers scurry after him, closing the gate. After a time his deep voice, measured, deliberate, washes over the congregation.

“Now, if you can behave like civilized human beings, come forward.”

Slowly the people in the pews nearest Magielda stand and move hesitantly, kneeling along the gleaming brass altar rail. When my turn comes to receive the ashes, I kneel as well. But I cannot look into the priest’s face and stare down at the shiny black serge of his cassock. A draft from the opened sanctuary door sweeps about me penetrating my thin coat and making me shiver against the clammy dampness of my shirt. When my turn comes to receive the ashes, I feel only a gritty thumb press quickly against my forehead in a gesture of repugnance and dismissal.

My mother and I emerge from the church's side entrance. A thin, tattered blanket of dirty snow lies about the yard between the church and the rectory. Through the holes jut angry clumps of coarse-bladed grass, inky colored in the winter shadows. As we walk along the bare pavement, frost-heaved and uneven, my mother quickens her pace. Lit by the purple light of the declining day, her face is a soft oval of opalescent white stained with the shapeless smudge of ashes on her forehead. Her hands are again tucked up into her sleeves and her shoulders thrust forward as if she would jostle anyone who dared impede our way. I watch as her eyes grow wide. Through pursed lips she spits out in a hoarse voice, "Hunh. Magielda didn't have to have a fit! Even if he is a priest, he ain't got the right to do that to the people."

At the end of the concrete walk, I reach for the brass handle of the door to the subway, a covered wooden stairway that leads to the street above. I grasp the cold metal, but I cannot get enough traction on the ice-covered walk, and I slip as the heavy door resists my attempt to open it. Angrily, and with a clumsy, twisting movement I wrench the door so that it bangs open against the stop. Wearily I follow my mother into the gloom of the unlit stairwell.